WELCOME

CREATIVITY IS INVENTING, EXPERIMENTING, GROWING, TAKING RISKS, BREAKING RULES, MAKING MISTAKES AND HAVING FUN.

— MARY LOU COOK

Our group of talented artists have truly lived up to Mary Lou Cook's definition of creativity. In the making of **DESIGNING WITH STAMPING**, they have done it all in regards to stamping. Through much experimenting and risk taking, they prove that stamping is not just for card making anymore. Come along as they dish up delightful ideas to incorporate stamping and ink into scrapbook pages and paper art projects— ideas that will encourage the beginner and challenge the experienced. Experiment, invent, break the rules and have fun as you discover a whole new world of stamping.

Pull up a chair and delight in dozens and dozens of delectable ideas that we hope will inspire you to use rubber stamps on your scrapbook pages and other paper art projects. A CD has been included with this book that contains even more projects, step-by-step instructions and a glossary of the terms used throughout the book. Let all these ideas help you put your personal "stamp" on every project you make.

THE AUTUMN LEAVES TEAM

TRACY KYLE

JENNIFER MCGUIRE

RENEE CAMACHO

LISA RUSSO

CAROL WINGERT

TENA SPRENGER

CATHY BLACKSTONE

LESLIE LIGHTFOOT

RHONNA FARRER

JENN BERTSCH

TINA BARRISCALE

SHARI CARROLL

PATRICIA ANDERSON

BECKY NOVACEK

JEN LESSINGER

ERIN TRIMBLE

CONTENTS

CHAPTER ONE

STAMPS

Rubber stamps have come a long way since their widespread use in the 1800's, when businesses used them for repetitive tasks. In this chapter, our artists take rubber stamps from the business world to the creative world and offer inspiring ideas of how to make custom stamps and how everyday objects can be transformed into ultra-cool "stamps" for your projects. You'll be repeating these innovative ideas over and over again when you discover the zing they can bring to your creations.

Stamp on Embellishments

ALPHABET FRAME
BY JENNIFER M.

Stamp on various surfaces with StazOn ink using several stamping techniques. Stamp on the wood frame with VersaMagic ink.

Mix Alphabets

BABY GIRL

BY TENA

Stamp name using tiny alphabet stamps on cardstock background. Stamp large "S" with VersaMark, sprinkle with embossing powder and heat emboss. Cut out embossed letter and mount on top of stamped background. To create the title block, stamp words using two sizes of alphabet stamps. Stamp larger letters with StazOn and stamp all other letters using clear embossing ink, then heat emboss all the words.

Cut out Stamped Alphabets

A MAMA AND HER LOVE

BY BECKY

Layer papers to make background. Add an oval label to a large tag, machine stitch bottom edge and tie with ribbon. Tuck tag under photo and tuck a smaller journaling tag under the other photo. Cut "S" spiral clips in half, and bend to form 3-D centers for the flowers. Stamp initials on cardstock, cut out and adhere to page. Add rick rack and ribbon to background and machine stitch down one side.

NOTE TO SELF

BY SHARI

Create a cast by setting a letter stamp–rubber side up–on a work surface. Place a piece of tissue paper over letter and spritz with water. Use a small, stiff paintbrush to push the tissue into crevices. Repeat. Fill in crevices with spackling compound to create firmness and durability. Continue adding layers of tissue until there are a total of five. Allow to dry. Trim and paint as desired.

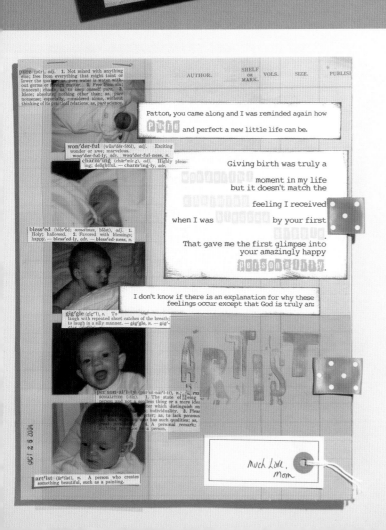

ARTIST

BY JENN B.

Print photos on a transparency. Cut words from the definition paper to create the journaling. Mix pigment ink colors on stamps and then stamp on a transparency.

FIRST DAY OF SCHOOL
BY CATHY

Zigzag stitch paper to background. Add a large photo over the top and stitch title to page. Stamp individual letters onto paper using brown ink. Use stickers, pogs or stencils for a few of the letters. Attach to page with photo turns and colored brads.

First Day of School

September 1, 2004
McVay Elementary
Kindergarten
Mrs. Davis

Stamp words directly on photos with StazOn ink. Stamp title onto ledger paper. Cut brackets out of blue patterned paper. Stamped number phrases between the negative bracket images with various stamps and inks.

Stamp on Photos

TIME WELL SPENT
BY TINA

hugs   laughs   kisses   secrets

TIME WITH YOU IS TIME WELL SPENT

FATHER & SON/WILLIAM & DADDY
ESTABLISHED:
2.1.01

3.75 YEARS
46months
1398 days   AS OF 11.28 2004
20l024omins   33504 HOURS
20,614,400 SECONDS

Create a Stamped Alphabet Background

COLE
BY RENEE

Stamp alphabet onto cardstock and cut out each letter individually. Attach to heavy cardstock background. Paint over entire surface, lightly coating each alphabet letter. Wipe off excess paint to create distressed background. Attach journaling strips on top of a fabric swatch.

Stamp on Different Surfaces

ABC'S OF BEING BOYS
BY JENN B.

Collage patterned papers onto cardstock. Attach a mini file folder to the cardstock so the back of the file folder is attached to the back of the layout. Ink the photos with a cotton ball swabbed with dye ink. Cut up definitions and staple to the pictures. Stamp the letters on fabric, cork and a tag. Attach the tag and cork with safety pins and ribbon. Adhere journaling to the inside of the file folder.

DEVOTED DANCER

BY JENNIFER M.

Heavily ink the front of a few paper doilies with pink chalk or pigment ink. Lay them ink side down onto white cardstock. While holding the doily still, use a brayer to transfer ink to the page. Keep one inked doily to embellish, heating to dry. Stamp a music staff on green strip with VersaMark. Adhere to page along with ribbons, photo and inked doily. Add embellishments and letters. Stamp text onto a paper flower and tuck flowers under metal word.

Stamp with a Bottle

JUST BE SILLY

BY BECKY

Add patterned paper to white cardstock to create background. With a paint sponge, apply paint to the opening of a clean and dry water bottle. Stamp circles on the corners of the background. Mat photos and ink the edges of the mat. Machine stitch around each mat, then affix to page.

RANDOM PICTURES
BY CATHY

Take a child's drawing to an office supply store and have the image turned into a custom rubber stamp. (Cathy's daughter drew the flower and it was turned into a stamp.) Stamp the flowers with dye ink onto kraft paper. Stamp the tops again on white paper, color with watercolor pencils, cut them out and adhere onto the kraft paper. Rip fabric, zigzag stitch near the edge and paint over the stitching. Use as a background for the photos.

Random pictures of you that I love taken during 2004 (they needed a home).

Stamp made from a flower that you drew for me.

SHOW CIRCLES
BY CAROL

To create spiral stamps, heavily ink a wire whisk with pigment-based ink (push the whisk into the ink pad) and then stamp onto paper. To create the "X" stitch, wrap waxed linen around a piece of a square craft wood. Ink "X's" with pigment ink and stamp over the seam line between two pieces of paper.

MANY THANKS
BY SHARI

To make the swirl, roll clay into a thin strand about 6" long and ¼" wide. Coil the strand starting from the center and move out. Place swirl on a non-stick surface to dry. When hardened, affix to foam mount with rubber cement. For the letters, roll clay into balls about the size of the stencils. Flatten evenly with a utensil. Press a metal stencil into the clay and let about ⅛" of clay come through. Allow to dry with metal stencil still attached. Gently remove stencils from hardened clay. Trim and adhere individual letters to foam pieces using rubber cement.

14

SOMEDAY
BY PATRICIA

Print title onto cardstock and cut out letters to create letter templates. Trace letters onto top of a mouse pad, then cut out. Adhere "stamps" to acrylic or wood block. Apply acrylic paint to letter stamps and press onto paper. To create layout, machine stitch green cardstock to white background. Stitch patterned paper over the top. Add photos and attach ribbon with staples and conchos. Adhere epoxy letters and cut out title. Staple journaling strips to layout.

You, Daddy and Ethan got these flowers for me.

Someday you'll give flowers to your girlfriend...

You know how much I love pink roses.

then to your wife, you'll make her so happy.

You look so handsome holding the flowers for me.

Someday you'll be grown, thankfully - not today.

NOAH
BY JEN L.

To make title, cut potatoes in half. Use a paring knife or other small knife to carve each letter on a different potato half, remembering to reverse the letter. Make the straight cuts first, then slowly make any rounded cuts. Use the same technique to carve the stick figures. Allow the potatoes to dry, then apply paint to the potatoes with a foam brush and stamp on cardstock. When dry, print journaling over the title.

IT IS HARD TO BE A LITTLE GUY.

BUTTERFLIES

BY JENNIFER M.

Cut a shape from corduroy. Adhere to wood or an acrylic block. Ink "stamp" with VersaMagic and stamp on paper. Embellish with machine stitches.

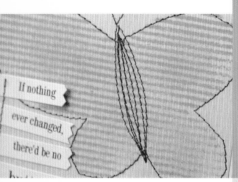

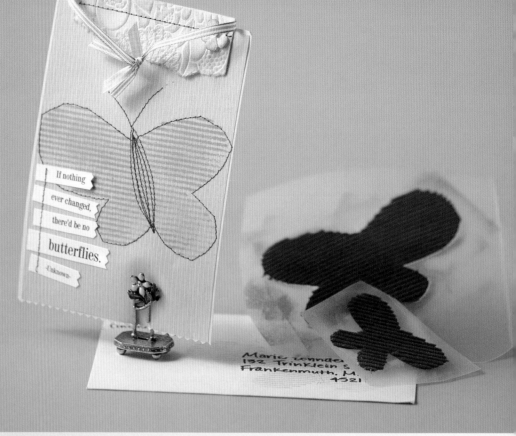

JOY

BY LISA

Print font on thin printer paper. Adhere to craft foam with removable adhesive and use a craft knife to cut out. Mount the letters on a ruler or on the back of another stamp, and stamp onto cardstock.

SARA AND CASE
BY JENN B.

Draw an image on the top of a cork and carve with X-Acto knife. Cork stamps make ideal travel stamps because they are so lightweight.

Shadow Stamp Behind Images

BLOCKED CARDS
BY CATHY

Stamp squares onto a strip of cardstock. Ink the edges, then adhere to card. Add silk flower with a button center and machine stitch a stem. Or machine stitch a heart over the stamped strip and add stamped letters.

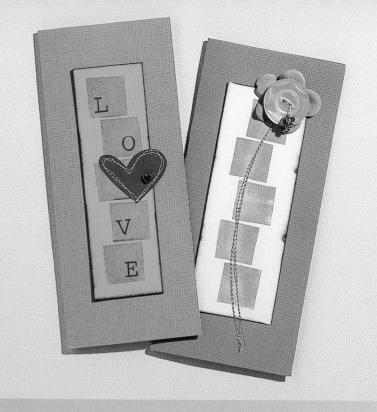

Resist Stamp Images

ZEST FOR LIFE
BY JENNIFER M.

Divide a two page spread into four sections with a light pencil line. Stamp various swirl images with VersaMark ink and clear emboss. Mask off one area and paint with acrylic paint. Wipe away excess to reveal the resisted embossed images. Do the same for the other three areas. For title, stamp on acrylic pieces with VersaMark and emboss in green. For "for life," write words with a VersaMark pen and heat emboss with green powder.

MY PARENTS
BY CAROL

Dye squares of canvas with color wash or use colored squares of fabric. Stamp image on fabric with ivory colored acrylic paint and allow to dry. Stamp over the same image with white gesso dabbed on parts of the stamp to create highlighted areas. Attach the squares to cardstock with fabric glue. Print photo on canvas or muslin, color wash or paint a frame around the photo and stamp around the perimeter. Attach buttons or charms to the center of each square and attach the photo with lace "hinges" which opens to reveal journaling.

MOMENTS
BY LESLIE

Use several stamping techniques on various types of papers. Cut into strips and stitch to black cardstock. Rub metal phrase with a white ink pad, making sure to get the ink into the grooves. Rub off the excess, heat set and add to layout. Frame title with a wooden frame and hang a charm from the frame.

STANDING AT THE EDGE
BY TINA

To create the background, measure out 2"x3" boxes (with ¼" spaces in between) across the two pages. Fill the extra spaces with a large photo on the left side and journaling on the right. In the remaining boxes, fill with stamped images, patterned paper and photographs. For the stamping, mask off each rectangle with four Post-it notes. Stamp image one or more times to completely fill the box. Stamp text over patterned paper rectangles. Cut metal rimmed tags to make large brackets. Hand cut title and adhere across the top of the page.

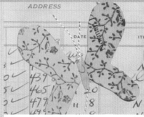

BUTTERFLY
BY RENEE

Using direct to paper technique, ink an assortment of found ledger and book papers. Stamp various images over inked pages and hand cut butterflies from assorted papers. Attach butterflies to page, creating trail marks and antennae with a sewing machine. Print journaling onto typing paper, leaving a space for the center of butterfly to be attached. Cut into a butterfly shape and adhere to page.

DAVID & MINNIE
BY TRACY

Rubber stamp on background patterned paper, mixing inks on the script stamp. Punch patterned papers into squares and attach to page. Rubber stamp the title and add accents to several of the squares.

23 DEGREES
BY JEN L.

To make the title, place stickers on white cardstock. Brayer blue ink over the top. Let dry and remove stickers with UnDu. Use temporary adhesive to adhere a large circle to white cardstock. Brayer green ink around the circle. Cut into a larger circle. Stamp snowflakes on the green with green ink. Mask off the green area and stamp bull's eye with blue ink. Adhere over background. Cut journaling into an arrow shape. Stamp blue circles over journaling, and layer over brayered green cardstock. Mat photo and frame date with a bookplate. Glue buttons to the center of the snowflakes.

SOMEDAY
BY TENA

To create the lace stamped image, press a piece of lace into VersaMark ink, then pressed it on the page. Roll over the top with a brayer. Sprinkle with embossing powder and heat emboss. Stitch photos and pieces from a pattern envelope. Idea to note: Try this technique with denim or another fabric with a texture that will show up when inked.

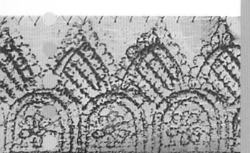

FRIENDS
BY SHARI

Use a glue dot to hold a bobbin to the work area. Coat the bobbin with paint. Press paper or a transparency to the bobbin. Punch into circles and affix to cards.

Stamp with Leaves
SAN DIEGO
BY CAROL

To create the fern patterned book cloth used to cover the accordion book, paint or lightly brayer acrylic paint onto the fronds of a live fern. Carefully place the fern—ink side down—onto the book cloth surface. Brayer over fern and lift carefully. Repeat the process with different sizes of ferns. Add coordinating paints to book plate, hemp and wooden bead.

Use your Fingerprints
SUNSHINE
BY JENNIFER M.

Ink fingers and use fingerprints to create the flower petals. Make background from various sizes of circles. Straight stitch several lines on the background. Use pop-dots to adhere some of the circles. Add buttons, page pebbles or paper flowers for the centers of the fingerprint flowers.

DINOSAURS
BY PATRICIA

Place letter stickers, toy dinosaur and leaves onto handmade paper. Spray with walnut ink. Remove toy and wash immediately. Let walnut ink dry, then remove letter stickers and leaves. Cut patterned paper to fit over part of the background, tear one side and ink the torn edge. Adhere to background, then punch three holes on the left side and tie with ribbon. Print journaling on a transparency and stitch to a walnut inked tag. Form a circle of clay and stamp a toy dinosaur foot into it. Bake as directed. When cool, apply ink to the footprint and affix to layout.

JUST BLOWIN' BUBBLES
BY LESLIE

Use a foam brush to spread acrylic paint over bubble wrap. Turn over and place on white cardstock to "stamp." Allow to dry. Cut stamped paper into strips and mix with other papers for the background. Machine stitch over a few seams. Highlight title with a circle die cut, adding yellow fabric paper behind the top circle. Embellish with a ribbon tie.

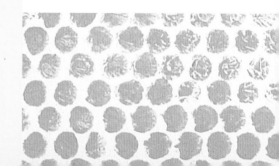

- hate to read (but do it well?)
- can tell a lie and eventually believe it
- can feel sick at the mention of a headache
- leave your clothes where they drop
- create your own dance moves
- talk forever and a day
- have an imagination that does not cease.
- build Bionicles all over the house
- give wedgies to your brother
- love to glue your hair (with gel of course)
- hate having Kaitlyn and Zachary follow you around
- love having a day away from your brother and sister

YOU

Stamp with a Dauber

YOU

BY RENEE

Ink several types of papers and stitch to background cardstock. Stitch
journaling strips to background. Stamp dots using a small stencil
dauber. Cover chipboard page corners and title letters with paper.

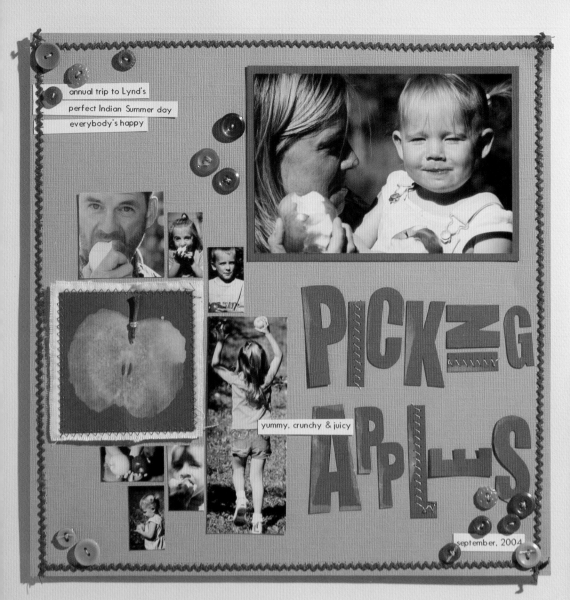

annual trip to Lynd's
perfect Indian Summer day
everybody's happy

yummy, crunchy & juicy

september, 2004

APPLE PICKING
BY CATHY

Cut an apple in half and allow to dry. Use bleach as the ink and stamp onto cardstock. Cut out title from cardstock and dip the edges in bleach. Zigzag stitch rick rack around the layout.

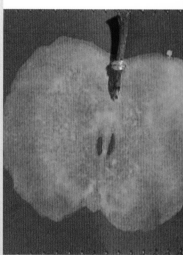

HAVE SPICES, WILL COOK
BY JEN L.

Print title and subtitle with computer. Create cross-hatch design by inking fork tines and pressing firmly onto white cardstock. Use scrap paper to mask the edge of the title. Do the first color in one direction, then do a second color in the opposite direction. Outline with ¼" strips of cardstock. Ink the edges with orange ink. Print spice names using blue text boxes and white text. Cut into circles and frame with conchos.

Have spices,
will cook.
[Please let them want something besides grilled cheese tonight!]

You love to cook. It is so unfair that Noah and I prefer food that doesn't need a lot of preparation. We like grilled cheese, quesadillas, pizza, sandwiches ... not much of a challenge for you. As the years have progressed, you have taken over a large chunk of the cooking duties in our family. I'm glad you like to do it, because I most certainly do not. Maybe someday we will surprise you and request some exotic dish that has 73 steps in the cookbook. But for tonight, how about a grilled cheese?

ginger   curry   cloves   pepper

Stamp on an adhesive lens sheet with StazOn ink. Cut out. Apply paint to hand and make print on cardstock. Add journaling to cardstock, attach photos and stamped lens accents. Paint chipboard letters. Use direct to paper technique with dye ink to make the "j" stencil green. Cover stencil with honeycomb ribbon and sponge dye ink over the top to make the dots. Stamp "y" and punch into a circle.

JOURNEY
BY TRACY

Life is a journey, and sometimes that journey is a bumpy ride. It seems like I have spent my whole life trying to figure out what and where I want to be...who I am supposed to be. I start out in one direction and realize that it is not where I want to be...start off in another direction and hope for the best. I spend so much time and energy searching for peace of mind...searching for contentment.

As a child I found myself overwhelmed with trying to please others. Frightened that if I did not please them I would not be loved. Focusing on achieving, pleasing, and always searching for love. Always searching for love, when it should have been right there. Always searching...my journey has started.

In the blink of an eye, I am a young adult. My focus was on where I could take myself and what I could do. Making money and material possessions were sought after. So much "real life" was passed by. So many years and so much effort spent going nowhere that I really wanted to go...I realized that was not who I wanted to be. Confused because this is who I was supposed to be. Craving peace of mind. Not sure how to get to the place that I want to be. Still on a personal journey.

Where has time gone, I find myself wondering. Making changes to focus less on who I am supposed to be and more of what I want to be. Sometimes feeling selfish...trying to focus on the important things in life. At 35 trying to find the magic place where everything will just fall in line. The place where everything will fell less like it is upside down. Focusing on family. Focusing on one day at a time. Still very much on my journey.

5, 20 and now 35...and still searching. Feeling like I am sometimes the only one that is searching. Waiting for someone to take hold of me and lead me to where I need to go. Trying to make a mark in life...trying to find purpose. I can close my eyes and see where I want to be 15 years from now...I certainly hope that I am on the right road.

DEC 4 2004

Tracy

BOGEY
BY JENN B.

To create the circle strip, dip the lid of a paint bottle into paint and stamp on white cardstock. Layer ribbons and paper to create a shrine effect for the photo.

Her function is to sit and be admired.

CHAPTER TWO

MEDIUMS

Anymore, stamping isn't just using a rubber stamp and an inkpad. The art of stamping now includes using ink with no stamps at all, finding different media to stamp with and experimenting with techniques such as resisting and embossing. Here, our artists employ ingenious media on their projects for dazzling results. And Rhonna achieves the stamped look on her pages without touching a stamp or ink—all through the expanding world of digital stamping. Gather your inks, paints, condensed milk (yes, you read that correctly), crayons, glue sticks, hot glue guns and bleach, and get ready to stamp in ways you've never imagined.

Stamp Melted Wax

BEAUTIFUL
BY JENN B.

With a stippling brush, cover the background paper with the antique linen ink. Adhere main photo. Melt wax in melting pot and use an old paint brush to apply wax to corner of the photo. Keep adding wax until it turns cloudy in appearance. Slightly heat the wax with a heat gun and place stamp in. Once the wax cools, remove the stamp, then swipe acrylic paint over the wax. Attach ribbon with conchos.

GLASS ORNAMENTS

BY TRACY

Apply alcohol ink to a piece of felt
and dab ink over surface of glass ball.
Different colors of inks can be layered for
a mottled effect. Add ribbons and charms
to top of ball.

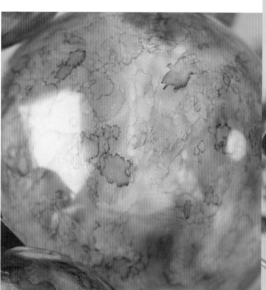

MERCY

BY JENNIFER M.

Score and fold a diamond pattern
with natural-colored cardstock. Using
a make-up applicator, rub ink on the
creases, using red, brown and green
ink. Tear edges along creases. Create
journaling on computer. Change the
color of the words that you want to
stamp to very light gray. Print out,
then stamp over the light gray letters.

DANDELION WISHES
BY TINA

Use a VersaMark reinker to draw the "scribbly" flowers on green paper. Sprinkle with clear embossing powder and heat emboss. Cut curves in the patterned paper and adhere to the background. Using photo editing software, print title directly on the photograph.

Dandelion WISHES

SOME CALL THEM FLOWERS OR EVEN WEEDS...YOU CALL THEM WISHES

Dye Fabric

MAKE EACH DAY COUNT
BY CAROL

To create fabric dyes, mix dye based reinkers with water. Add enough ink concentrate to make a fairly dark color because the color fades as the cloth dries. Add pieces of fabric such as ivory linen, matelasse, canvas, etc. The dye penetrates the fabric better if the fabric has been thoroughly pre-wet with hot water. Allow the fabric to soak in the dye until it appears to have the desired intensity and hang to dry.

To create a paint which coordinates with the shades of ink used on paper or fabric, pour white gesso into a small plastic cup. Add dye reinker (same type as mentioned above) several drops at a time until the desired shade of paint is achieved. Paint over sanded metal accents, paper, chipboard, etc.

Pumpkin patch trip - October 2003

GRAND TOTAL.

Kaitlyn misses you this year. You've started Kindergarten and left her at home. What's a little sister who is so used to having her big brother around to do during the day other than make messes? Nothing seems to be exciting. Mom sure isn't exciting. Mom is really rather boring when compared to the antics that you played for Kaitlyn each day. You kept Kaitlyn's life busy and exciting during her toddler years to this point. And now, you're gone. It seems that nothing will take our place. But, as the year progresses, I'm sure that eventually boredom will become comfortableness in a newfound independence that you being in Kindergarten will provide for her. In the meantime, Kaitlyn will just enjoy experiencing the little moments of Kindergarten visits and field trips and having something to look forward to. Like a school field trip to the pumpkin patch. Just know that you've always got someone looking up to you, Zachary, someone who loves you VERY much!

Kaitlyn · 3
Zachary · 5
Mrs Thomas

Rub Ink on Papers

I MISS YOU
BY RENEE

Mask off stripes of various sizes by using a low-tack tape. Rub inkpads directly over taped-off areas to create stripes. Emboss some of the stripes for more texture. Add machine stitches to a few "seams." Create stripes on the stencil letters following the same steps as the background.

Ink with a Mask

V & A
BY LISA

Adhere die cut or hand cut letters to background cardstock with a removable adhesive. Mask off various-shaped spaces and fill with pigment ink rolled on with a sponge-paint trim roller. Remove letters.

VIC AND AIDAN - AUGUST 2004

Ya think they look alike? From the day Aidan was born, everyone said "He looks JUST like Vic!" The round head, the blue eyes, the thick hair, the stocky build. I've done pages about this before, but it's nice to show it now that they're both a little older.

This picture was taken at Rock City in Tennessee. Vic took pictures of Aidan with me, in which he refused to do anything but pose like a goof (typical). Then I had him pose with Vic, and he immediately settled in to show his love for his Daddy. Warms the cockles of my heart, whatever those are. I realize the days of all-mommy-love are headed out, but at least I get to watch my two lookalikes bond. Which is a sweet thing, indeed.

DAISIES
BY LESLIE

Fill a spray bottle with ink from a reinker; dilute slightly with water. Spray onto white textured cardstock and crinkle, then flatten before it dries. Create background with cardstock and strips of patterned paper. Accent with machine stitches on some of the seams. Add journaling and photos to layout. Sew on buttons and adhere printed twill. Cut title into individual pieces and affix to page.

KISS
BY TRACY

Using a brayer and dye ink, roll inks onto glossy cardstock and wipe to blend. Stamp images over parts of the brayered cardstock. Punch into squares. Spray color wash inks over squares. Attach squares to page, using foam strips on some to add dimension. Stamp plastic circles with StazOn ink and attach to page.

Acrylic Paint Stamping

REAL BOY
BY LESLIE

Spray white textured cardstock with walnut ink. Adhere strips of patterned paper to the left side of layout.

Using acrylic paint as the ink, rubber stamp on cardstock and fabric paper. Accent the photo and a few blocks with stitching. Stamp circles on scraps, cut out and adhere to page.

To become a real boy you must prove yourself brave, truthful, and unselfish.
Pinocchio

Keaton (age 3) ...and one hundred percent REAL. Brave always (you sure do scare me with all your crazy stunts!) Truthful to a fault ("Mommy, I hit Chloe!") Unselfish most of the time... unless it means sharing with your sis!

Stamp into Clay

TENDER LOVING CARE
BY JENNIFER M.

Flatten clay to about ¼" thick. Press un-inked heart stamp or letter stamps into the clay. Use mini cookie cutter to cut clay into circle shape, then bake according to manufacturer's instructions.

Incredibly touching...
tender hearted people...
...spending hours tending to graves of others...
...making this Salzburg
cemetery heaven on earth...
...a loving expression of devotion...
...an example of unselfish care.
Pure tender loving care.

Salzburg.
One of my favorite
places on earth.

SO ALIVE
BY JENNIFER M.

Paint condensed milk on a stamp, then stamp onto paper. Heat generously with a heat gun until it browns. Add a bit of color with colored pencils.

I have never felt as alive as I did on this day, driving through Austria. Austria's hills are so amazing... full of magical color, winding roads, tranquil lakes and fresh air. We stopped often to take pictures to try and capture the magic. No wonder it was this heavenly area that inspired the lyrics...

"The hills are alive..."

so alive

QUILTED FRIENDS CARDS
BY SHARI

Sponge bleach onto a stamp with a make-up applicator. Stamp onto fabric. Dry with a heat gun. Quilt fabric together and hand sew buttons and notions in place.

PINKY SWEAR
BY TRACY

Place a piece of vellum over rubber stamp and rub with crayon. Cut out. Attach images with clear adhesive.

This technique works best with stamps that do not have fine details.

Stamp with Glue and Leafing

THANK HEAVEN
BY JENNIFER M.

Apply a Zig glue stick to the rubber of a stamp. Stamp onto paper. If it doesn't give a full stamped image, fill in with the glue stick. Let dry completely. Once dry, press leafing into the dry glue (which will be sticky) and use a stencil brush to remove excess. For flower vase, print message on transparency, cut into vase shape and sew onto layout, tucking flowers inside.

Searching for the perfect Christmas tree
Gigantic snowflakes began to fall
They were so big that it seemed unreal

It was magical

Jackson saw no fun or beauty in this
I began the negotiating procedures with him
Lost sight of you
Then I turn around to find you and there you are

Doing what you are supposed to be doing.

2003

CATCHING SNOWFLAKES
BY CATHY

Print enlarged photo onto linen cardstock. Stamp snowflakes with bleach on blue cardstock. Cut out, then rub each edge of the snowflake squares with bleach. Zigzag stitch squares around the perimeter of the layout.

MY DAD
BY TENA

To use printer's type stamps, first clean the stamps well, ink with a moist inkpad and press firmly onto the surface of the project. The metal stamps have no "give," so press firmly to get a good impression.

On a firm surface, position metal stamp onto metal and give a few firm taps with a small hammer to make the impression. To highlight the words, rub StazOn ink over the top of the metal, rubbing away excess ink on the surface while allowing it to stay in the stamped letters.

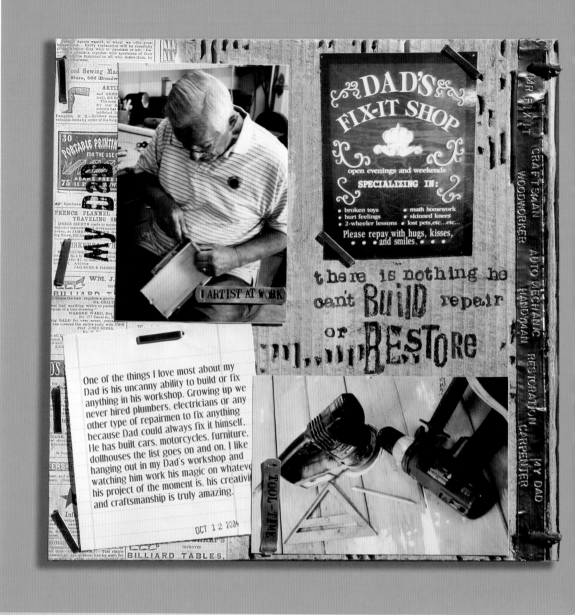

One of the things I love most about my Dad is his uncanny ability to build or fix anything in his workshop. Growing up we never hired plumbers, electricians or any other type of repairmen to fix anything because Dad could always fix it himself. He has built cars, motorcycles, furniture, dollhouses the list goes on and on. I like hanging out in my Dad's workshop and watching him work his magic on whateve his project of the moment is, his creativi and craftsmanship is truly amazing.

OCT 1 2 2004

BABY CARDS AND ENVELOPE
BY PATRICIA

Using acrylic paint as the ink, stamp flowers onto cards and on the back of envelope. Let dry. Run paint along sides of cards. Using the flat end of a foam paint brush, paint dots in the centers of the flowers. Let dry and apply rub-on words.

BABY NO MORE
BY PATRICIA

Mix powdered dye with water to get desired color. Dip foam stamps into thin layer of dye, then press onto white cardstock. Let dry, then cut out letters. Stamp #5 onto a walnut inked tag. Create background grid from cardstock and patterned papers. Cover the paper seams with strips of leather paper. Staple letters to layout and slide tag under photo.

RESIST TAGS
BY SHARI

Stain printed papers with a light wash of instant coffee using a make-up wedge sponge. Set aside to dry. Clear emboss images onto stained papers. Using a clean wedge, apply a wash of blue dye (liquid ink) over embossed images and set aside to dry. Sandwich the prepared papers between a sheet of blank newsprint and iron on a hot setting until melted embossing powder appears on the top sheet. Assemble as desired.

Brayer on Ink

WISH FRAMES
BY TRACY

For the "w" and "s", reverse print letter on the back of glossy cardstock. Stamp images on the front with resist ink. Brayer dye or chalk ink over the top and wipe off excess to reveal images. Cut out letter and attach to cardstock with foam strips. For the "i" and "h", stamp images with resist ink on glossy cardstock. Brayer dye or chalk ink over the top and wipe off excess to reveal images. Reverse print letter on the back of cardstock. Cut out letter and attach to resist background with foam strips.

SMILE

BY JENNIFER M.

Stamp various images onto glossy paper using VersaMark ink. Let dry completely or heat to dry. Start in one corner and cut out one small piece. Lay over scrap paper. Generously dab a make-up applicator onto dye ink and rub generously over glossy piece. Adhere to corner of another 12"x12" background piece. (This piece will just hold it all together.) Cut another piece from the glossy paper and rub with a different color of ink. Continue to cut pieces of various sizes, inking and adhering to background.

SIMPLE JOYS

BY JENNIFER M.

Stamp flower images on white cardstock with VersaMark ink. Sprinkle with clear embossing powder and heat set. Generously apply watercolor over images and buff with a paper towel for resist effect.

THE QUIET AFTERNOON
BY RENEE

Paint entire canvas background with khaki paint. Add drops from a wax crayon using a heat tool. Paint over entire portion of canvas with thinned blue acrylic paint. Remove wax drippings to show resist areas. Attach book page, photos and accents.

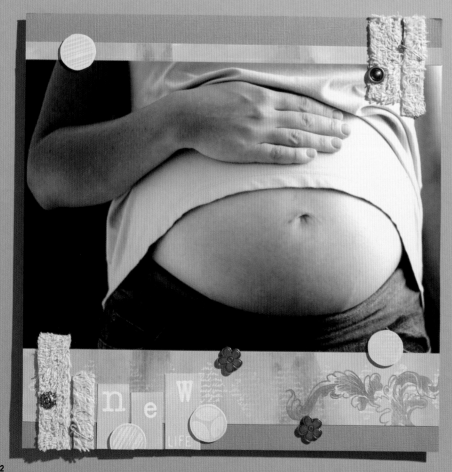

NEW LIFE
BY TRACY

Stamp images onto glossy cardstock with resist ink. Using a brayer, randomly apply different colors of ink. Cut out circle images and cut a strip for the border. Adhere chenille with double-sided tape and add decorative brads for interest.

CARDS AND FOLIO

BY CAROL

Using clear embossing ink, stamp image on watercolor paper and clear emboss. Paint over entire piece of watercolor paper with a color wash. This may take several applications to darken the color sufficiently. Clear stamp and clear emboss same image next to first image. When dry, color wash entire paper again. Repeat two more times. Let dry, then apply to the front of a folio, add coordinating paper, ribbons and decorative corners.

To create the cards, clear emboss and color wash images to coordinate with folio. To remove the shiny surface from the resist area, place image face down between two sheets of copy paper and press with a hot iron (no steam). Iron quickly and lift the card immediately so it doesn't stick to the paper.

ART SCHOOL—HERE I COME!

BY JEN L.

Print "art" on glossy photo paper. Make random scribbles with a white crayon. Rub blue pigment ink over the top, then wipe with a paper towel. Circle punch title letters. Print the rest of the title and journaling on white cardstock. Cut into a curve and attach to blue background. Adhere a matted photo. Stamp on a library pocket and staple to layout.

43

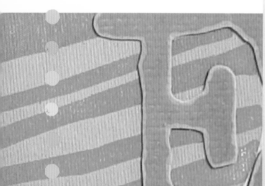

EVERY
BY TRACY

Stamp letters with VersaMark, emboss with clear powder and cut out. Stamp images with VersaMark, emboss and cut into circle shapes. Print journaling, cut out circle shapes and attach to page.

every moment
every look
every word
every gesture
every touch
every gaze
every thought
every movement
every detail

every reason
to love you

♥ Mom

EVERY

MUCH BETTER
BY JENNIFER M.

Print title on transparency. While still wet, shake on white embossing powder and heat set. Stamp on cardstock strips with VersaMark. Heat emboss with white or colored embossing powder.

just like me... only much, much better.

Devoted

never raises his voice to me

loves his bowl of ice cream every night

couldn't tell you the name of 5 current athletes

genuine

things I want you to know about your **dad**

hypnotized by TV

pack rat

has this quirky little happy dance that he does when he loves the food he's eating

uses the expressions, "phooey" and "rats" frequently

rubs his toes together while watching TV

he has never been mean towards ANYONE since i have known him

laughs hardest when watching, "who's line is it anyway?"

cried hardest when putting Max down

truly the best dad I know

AUTHENTIC

THINGS I WANT
YOU TO KNOW
BY CATHY

Clear emboss stamped images, then rub with metallic rub-ons. Sand the edges of the photographs and rub ink over the sanded areas. Round a few of the photos' corners.

C: I LOVE YOU

BY LESLIE

Color block papers to create background. To make the stencil accent, lightly dip a letter stencil into white pigment ink. Sprinkle with embossing enamel and heat emboss. Dip stencil in clear embossing ink, sprinkle with embossing enamel and heat set. Repeat with clear embossing ink over and over. In between some layers, add the metal accents, then add more layers on top. On the final layer, sprinkle the top with frosty white glitter, then heat emboss to trap glitter within the accent.

Chloe Raine Lightfoot
One Year Old

"Sweet C"... you are such an amazing little girl. I look at you and I melt. I think of you and I smile. You are just a dream ...with your calm disposition and your easy ways. You are such a happy baby and completely at peace with 'your' world. I am one lucky mom to call you my daughter. You make me proud, you bring me joy and I love you!

MINE

BY LISA

Print text on vellum in various shades of grayscale. Immediately after removing from printer, shake on clear embossing powder and brush off excess. Gently heat emboss, moving the heat gun constantly to prevent warping or burning. Attach over background cardstock with punched and stamped embellishment underneath.

FUN IN THE SUN
BY PATRICIA

Layer patterned papers to form background. Stamp title onto photo, apply white embossing powder and heat set. Hand stitch around the embossed title. Stamp flowers onto a transparency, heat emboss with white embossing powder, then cut out. Print journaling onto a transparency and tear along left side. Rub the edge with ink, apply white embossing powder and heat set. Attach journaling to a walnut inked tag with three tacks. Adhere photos, tag and embossed flowers to page.

YOUR BROTHERS
BY RENEE

Dry emboss leaf accents onto kraft-colored cardstock. Turn over embossed images and place stencil on top of raised surface. Coat the surface with clear embossing ink, remove the stencil, then heat emboss with clear embossing powder to create a shiny, raised surface. Print journaling onto ledger paper and attach to background. Create swatches of paint for leaf backgrounds. Sew around paint accents. Attach photos and cut out embossed leaves with pop dots.

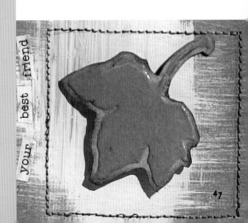

Create Faux Accents

JKF

BY RHONNA

Create the stone accents by using distressed brushes and burning them into the surface to give depth. Next, apply a texture filter of "sandstone" to the areas (scaling 69%, relief 4%). To create the rough edges on the stone, "erase" with a distress brush and apply a drop shadow style to give depth and dimension. Choose a font that will lend itself to the stamping texture on the sandstone. Use type tool to type onto the stone for the stamped effect.

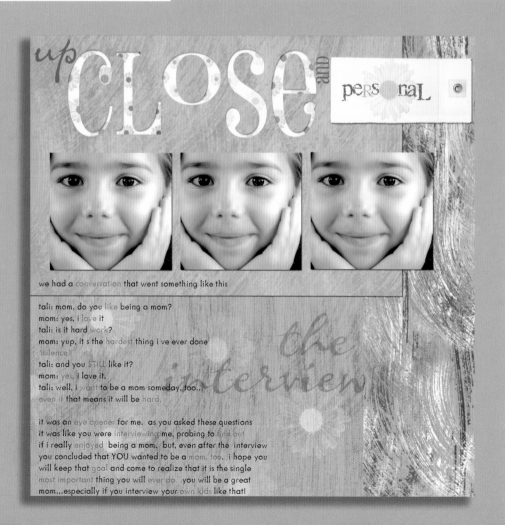

Use Filters for Texture

UP CLOSE & PERSONAL

BY RHONNA

Create the fabric look by applying various texture filters. To create the green fabric and tag, use the canvas filter. Using a flower brush, "stamp" flowers onto the tag and green fabric. Using a brushstroke brush, "stamp" color and texture onto the right side of the green fabric.

MEXICO
BY RHONNA

Create alphabet brushes and stamp them onto a digital acrylic plate. To create the brushes, select a font, edit by transforming size, rotate (to give some variation and the appearance of real stamps) and "erase" with a distress brush to give a stamped look. Digitally create an acrylic plate (for directions, see the credits page). Stamp text onto the acrylic plate.

SCHOOL
BY RHONNA

Create various brushes of scrolls, swirls and brush strokes. Use the dodge tool to lighten the brush strokes into the background papers. Use the burn tool to burn the scrolls and swirl brushes into the background papers.

SISTERLY LOVE
BY RHONNA

To make fonts look like stamped letters, stamp "sisters" at the bottom of the page by using the Overlay Light Mode at 34% opacity. Warp "sisterly love" at an arc of 79%. Work in different angles (warped arc, vertical, or dividing words to create horizontal and vertical journaling) and use different colors when using several fonts to get a hand-applied stamped look. The type is created by using the type tool, then rasterizing the layer and using various distress brushes to erase the fonts, giving it a stamped effect.

Create Resist-Like Images

HAPPINESS
BY RHONNA

Choose a design brush. Using the erase tool, erase the area to give a resist look. Apply a bevel and emboss style to the positive space which will make the "resist" stamping appear dimensional and will allow anything that was created underneath to show through.

M

BY RHONNA

Create slide mounts, clear dots and plate by applying a Style (see credits section for full directions). Use a textured brush to "erase" edges of the slide mounts. Use a colored design brush to stamp onto the clear plate, apply bevel & emboss style to give dimension and depth. Apply type tool over the top.

MY EVERYTHING

BY RHONNA

Create the vellum look by adjusting layer to 34% opacity. Apply a floral brush over the top of the vellum. Apply a bevel and emboss style to the brush layer (see credits).

CHAPTER THREE

SURFACES

If it's not moving, these artists will stamp on it! Everything from metal and glass to silk flowers and rubber bands have proven to be super surfaces for stamping. This chapter is all about going beyond paper and exploring a variety of surfaces for stamping or inking. You'll fall in love with how Jennifer transforms clear buttons into endearing embellishments and how Renee stamps on fabric to make a heartwarming creation. Take this hobby to the next level by stamping on some unsuspecting surfaces.

Stamp on Wood

REMEMBER
BY TRACY

Enlarge photo to 8"x12" and attach to page. Stamp images onto wood tags with StazOn ink. Let dry completely. Cut strips of cardstock and fabric and attach to page. Tie tags with ribbon and add flower and page pebble embellishments.

Remember
this moment

It was the last day at the lake. The evenings were getting cooler and we knew it was our sign to head home, yet we were reluctant to have our vacation end. The time that Tristan, Isabella and I spend at the lake is precious to us all. It is the time when we focus on just playing and enjoying each other's company, as there are no distractions. It is the time when it is OK to stay up late and take our blanket to the beach and just lay on our backs and watch stars. It is the time when we sit and read stories together and it seems we never get out of our bathing suits. We go and dangle our feet off the edge of the dock just one more time... and know that next summer we can do it all over again.

enjoy

AUG 1 4 2004

Stamp on Leather

THE HIKE
BY RENEE

Stamp dot image onto leather using StazOn. Trace flower onto stamped leather and cut out. Heat edges of leather with a wood-burning tool to burn and curl them up. Stamp dot image onto cardstock squares, placing flower on top. Back clear buttons with patterned paper and attach to flower using twist ties. Attach a walnut-inked tag to one of the twist ties. Stitch the layered accent to the page. Stitch two pieces of cardstock to background to form the photo mat. Stamp a weave pattern onto leather and cut to form photo corners. For the title, stitch wooden letters to the page with waxed linen.

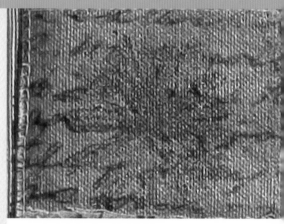

Stamp With Metallic Paints

COLLECTIONS FOLIO
BY CAROL

Paint canvas squares with textile paint and allow to dry. Using various stamps and metallic paint colors, stamp over the top. When dry, stitch onto a larger piece of stamped and stenciled fabric. Use to cover a collections folio constructed from kraft gift bags.

To create the folio, cut the handles off three kraft gift bags. Fold each bag in half, then place each bag on top of the other, alternating the side of the opening. Using an in-and-out stitch, hand stitch together on the fold line. Glue covers onto front and back of "book."

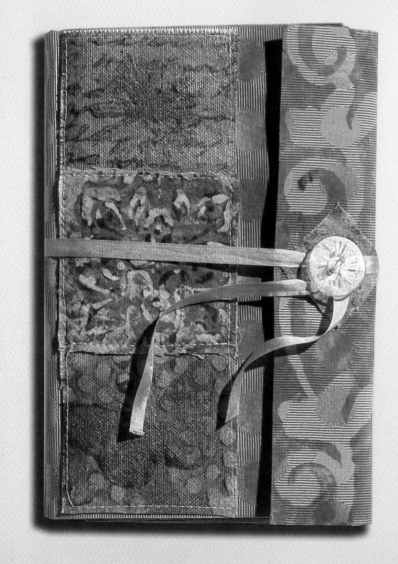

FRIEND

BY JENNIFER M.

Cut fabric pieces into diamond shapes. Stamp with assorted colors on the diamond pieces and on ribbon. On the silk, heat set immediately to prevent bleeding. On dark colors, use white Brilliance ink and emboss with white powder. Adhere diamonds to cork, adding ribbon in between. Add pins for accents.

COURAGE
BY RENEE

Stamp various images onto fabric swatches. Piece fabric swatches together in a quilt-like fashion onto a solid cardstock background. Top stitch together using a zigzag stitch and cut out. Cut out individual stamped title letters, adhering over scraps of stamped fabric pieces.

it takes courage to grow up and become who you really are
- e e cummings

Personality...this is something that you and I have been blessed with. It's something that we just exude naturally. We have a lot of "personality". Some call it spunk. Some call it vivaciousness. Some call it attitude. Some call it an 'outstanding' temperament. I choose to call it personality. This is something that I have struggled with my entire life. I have always tended to regret what I have said, to regret how I've acted and responded. I've had to learn to accept certain things in my life. I used to try so hard to be a person that I wasn't, and try to be that calm, demure, docile personality that others wanted me to be. Finally, a few years ago, I realized that in order for me to become a better person that I was going to have to stop trying to be something that I could never be and embrace the person that I was. I will say that in that moment (and the several that followed) I learned that I could semi-control myself. I could contain my personality when the circumstances called for it. Have I gotten better? I hope so...I think so? I hope that by the time you are ready to contain your own energetic personality that is so much like my own that I will have so many more lessons under my belt to share with you. I want to be able to teach you to be a good person, having that personality that will surely make you shine, but still containing it so it doesn't infringe upon others...this is my goal...to teach you the courage to be yourself.

Photo taken by Brandon August 12, 2004

COURAGE

CITY GIRL
BY BECKY

Stitch fabric to background paper. Add a layer of patterned paper over the top. Stitch photo to fabric and adhere to layout. Stamp sunflowers onto twill and stitch to layout. Stamp an "A" on a fabric scrap and frame with a canvas frame trimmed with tassel. Tuck silk flowers under twill.

You are a city girl. A visit to Pop and Mimi's at the lake is a *back to nature* experience for you. Picking wild sunflowers by the river was quite an adventure.

SOME PEOPLE MARCH TO A DIFFERENT DRUMMER — AND SOME PEOPLE POLKA

Isabella often drives me absolutely insane with her need to be different. Always dressing in "her" style. Always doing things "her" way. Always 180 degrees from everyone else. I will never have to worry about her wanting to following the crowd because she will always be doing her own thing, her own way, at her own speed and although it annoys me, it is one of my favourite Isabella traits.
August 2007

POLKA
BY TRACY

Using spray adhesive, attach fabric to cardstock pieces, then cut in random shapes. Rubber stamp flowers on top with dye ink and hand stitch the center. Stamp flowers on cardstock and stitch the centers as well. Cut around the flowers with a craft knife and bend the petals up for dimension.

Create Impressions in Velvet

REMEMBER EVERYDAY
BY SHARI

To stamp on velvet, set rubber stamp onto ironing surface with rubber facing up. Mist velvet with water and place velvet—fuzzy side down—onto the rubber stamp. Place a sheet of paper over the velvet and iron gently (on a hot setting with no steam) for a couple of seconds. Turn stamped velvet into a button with an upholstery button kit. Stamp directly onto leather using dye ink and use a button kit to complete. Stamp a message onto silk with StazOn.

DRAGONFLY
BY CATHY

Stitch fabric onto a square of cardstock. Stamp a large dragonfly so it bleeds off the fabric onto the cardstock. Stitch a strip of striped paper down the side for added color.

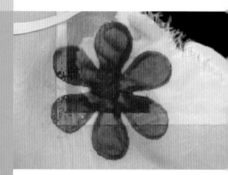

SILJE
BY PATRICIA

Stamp flowers with acrylic paint onto a triangular piece of organza (use a piece of paper under the fabric to protect the surface). Let dry. Run paint along edges of taupe cardstock. Let dry. Adhere photos, journaling strips and moulding to layout. Add organza to bottom corner. Hand stitch beads onto the organza all the way through cardstock. For the title, type name in WordArt, then flip name, print and cut out. Adhere over organza.

COWBOY IN THE JEANS

BY JENN B.

Adhere a denim strip over background paper. Stamp images on the denim with acrylic paint. Add photo and a smaller denim strip near the top. Accent with ribbon and a snap. Paint the cover of 7gypsies album and book board piece with acrylic paint, then distress with brown dye ink. Stamp "cowboy" onto cardstock, cut out each letter and swipe with brown ink. Print the rest of the title and accent with ink. Adhere both to the book board. Stamp partial images on a scrap of denim and adhere to book board. Attach journaling to album cover. Tie the cover on with ribbon and attach the book board with hinges.

Stamp on Clear Buttons

TRADEMARK EXPRESSION

BY JENNIFER M.

Stamp on clear buttons with StazOn ink. Arrange assorted buttons to create a page border.

Audrey's Trademark Expression. How stinkin' cute is it? We see this face often. It usually follows one of the following events:

· Kay bossing her around.   · Trying to catch the Frisbee, but missing.
· Dad telling her "no."   · Uncle Mike teasing her about something.
· Mum taking another photo.   · Not being able to wear red sparkle shoes to the store.

What a doll. Summer 2004. Age 6½

Audrey's expression™

Stamp on Vellum

DO YOUR PART

BY RENEE

Stamp various images onto colored vellum using StazOn ink. Cut into petals and adhere to page around a vellum quote trimmed into a circle. Cut a stem from vellum, stamping additional information using alphabet stamps and StazOn ink. Sew around circle and stem to securely attach vellum.

cute & sweet

Katie

CUTE & SWEET

BY TRACY

Stamp images on shrink plastic with StazOn, punch holes in the center and shrink with a heat gun until flat. Tie shrink plastic "buttons" and other embellishments to a cardstock strip.

ENJOY EVERY MOMENT

BY LISA

Using a word-processing program, create several overlapping text boxes. Fill the boxes with words and quotes, altering the fonts, sizes and text shading. Print on gray cardstock. Cut four evenly-spaced circles. Back two with photos and one with journaling printed on patterned paper. For the fourth circle, stamp a clock image on a clear CD using StazOn ink. Attach with a decorative brad.

GIRL TALK

BY TENA

Using StazOn ink, stamp images onto glass microscope slides. To prevent the slide from breaking when stamping, stamp on a surface with a little bit of give such as a magazine. Adhere colored cardstock to the back of the slides. To support the weight of the slides, mount layout on chipboard.

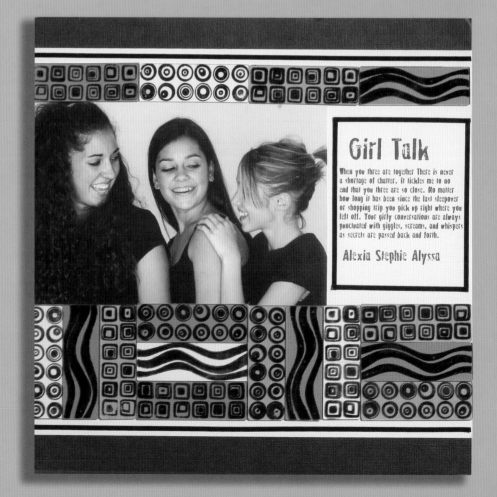

62

THE "NO" PA...

THOMAS
AGE 1

The word "no" echoes through the halls of our home, repeatedly, continually. Yet, you are oblivious to it, I suspect that it is a case of selective hearing. If anything, the word emboldens you, to run faster, to climb higher, to outwit your parents. At sixteen months, I would classify you as fearless, with an insatiable curiosity, and an astute ability to create chaos. I try to temper my usage of "no" to only situations of impending peril, yet it seems to be somewhat instinctual on the part of a parent. Initially, I wondered if you did not understand the meaning of the word, but only for a second. For you have deftly learned to shake your head to express your displeasure and are just now starting to articulate the word itself. You certainly know what it means and you express the sentiment, multiple times daily. And that my son, is the ultimate irony. The "no" paradox.

Stamp on Clear Stickers

THE "NO" PARADOX
BY TINA

Design title in word-processing program. Print title in reverse on the paper backing of translucent sticker paper. Hand cut the letters with an X-Acto knife. Ink stamp with StazOn ink and stamp over the entire surface of each letter. Remove backing from the letters and adhere to a printed transparency. Add additional letter stickers and rub-ons to complete title. Print journaling on photo paper using a black text box and white text.

Layer Embossed Transparencies

CELEBRATE CARD
BY JENNIFER M.

Create an accordion-folding card from kraft cardstock. While folded, cut a window through all layers. Sew transparencies to the backs of the windows. Stamp messages onto each window with VersaMark and emboss with various colors, scattering their placement so they all show through when closed.

Create a Stamped Frame

FRIENDS
BY SHARI

Using a glue stick, cover a photo mat with tissue paper. Use fine grit sandpaper to slightly distress the covered frame. Stamp images using chalk inks. Stamp "friends" text onto a laminate chip with black StazOn.

Stamp on Silk Flowers

FINE LINE
BY JENNIFER M.

Pluck flowers from plastic stems and remove centers. Stamp flowers with pigment or dye ink. Add buttons to the center and hand-stitch flower stems.

MILK
BY TRACY

Trace a large circle onto yellow cardstock and cut out. Attach to background. Tear fabric into strips, cut cardstock into strips and attach to background along with photos. Repeatedly print "milk" onto cardstock, cut into a strip and attach. Stamp on mirrors with StazOn, then adhere to page.

Create Stamped Jewelry

NECKLACE
BY JENNIFER M.

Dab style stones with yellow chalk ink. Heat to dry. Stamp various stamped images with chalk ink and heat again. Add letters, beads and ribbon.

65

GRANDMA'S BOYS
BY JENN B.

Paint chipboard to create background. Staple ribbon onto tags. Adhere photos, tags and patterned paper strips to background. To create the mini album, fold an envelope around the edge of the layout, cut halfway down two sides so it opens up. Use an elastic band to hold extra photos inside.

Stamp on Chipboard

WRAPPED BOXES
BY JENNIFER M.

Paint heavy chipboard pieces with acrylic paint. Let dry. Stamp the pieces with various images using chalk ink and heat to dry. Add ribbon.

OH BABY BABY IT'S A WILD WORLD

WILLIAM AGE 3

I watch as you spin the globe around on its axis, sometimes slowly, thoughtfully, other times vigorously. Your curiosity is piqued but the shapes, the colours, the animal symbols. You can easily identify, Ottawa (where we live now), Saskatoon, and Victoria (where your grandparents reside). You can find England with the guidance of London Bridge and peculiarly you can always identify Japan. As you study the globe I speculate about your future. Where will you travel, where will you live, what will you see? Although the protective mother in me wishes she could keep you safe and close to home, I wish for you a life of freedom, of exploration. Behold the beauty of our planet, experience other cultures and customs, embrace adventure, revel in nature. Protect our oceans, our air, our animals. Put back into the earth, what you take from it. For you are a steward for future generations. Our magnificent world depends on you.

HE'S GOT THE WHOLE

WORLD IN HIS HANDS

WILD WORLD
BY TINA

Stamp the hemisphere stamp on the front of acrylic tiles with black StazOn ink. Add rub-ons to two of the tiles over the stamped image. Layer the acrylic tiles over photos of the globe. Make a title from stamped letters and letter stickers. Print journaling onto cardstock and secure photos. Affix number stickers to clear buttons and layer over photos of the globe. Staple ribbons to the page and place buttons over the top.

GRIN
BY TRACY

Stamp laminate chips with StazOn ink. Paint chipboard letter "r" and let dry. Stamp with dot stamp. Attach printed transparency to background. Attach paper behind epoxy letter "n". Stitch buttons to layout.

You can accomplish a lot with a big grin.

Alex & Mackenzie 2003

THE SIMPLE STUFF
BY RENEE

White wash chipboard background with acrylic paints. Apply Texture Magic over a stencil form. Allow to dry, then ink several colors over top portions by placing stencil over textured surface again. Then stamp the images with additional images. Stitch textured and patterned papers on top.

The easeful days, the dreamless nights;

The homely round of plain delights;

The calm unambitioned mind,

The simple stuff of summer time.

—Aster Austin Dobson

Summer 2004 nature photos (Cheekwood)

SAND & SEA
BY CAROL

Using foam letter stamps, stamp with paint onto sandpaper. Allow to dry. Cut out letters and adhere to book cover. To create textured and bleached letters, sprinkle sand randomly onto a piece of cardstock. Using bleach, stamp foam letters over the sandy texture. Lift carefully. Allow to dry then brush off sand particles.

PENSACOLA BEACH

BY JENN B.

Stamp flower on the transparency sheet with pigment ink, sprinkle with embossing powder and heat emboss for a raised effect. Stamp "Pensacola" and "beach" on a transparency, then cut to fit on top of the layout.

Stamp and Dry Emboss Metal

THE ONE PERSON

BY JENNIFER M.

Stamp images on back of metal. When dry, dry emboss the images on soft surface. Flip metal over and adhere to layout. Cut metal for #1 and add word strips to complete title.

69

Stamp on Rubber Bands

RUBBER GREETINGS
BY SHARI

Stamp letters onto rubber bands using StazOn ink. Use as embellishments on cards.

Combine VersaMark with Chalk

MY WORLD
BY CAROL

For the first page, print a photo onto Sheer Heaven paper. Stamp image onto border with VersaMark ink and apply chalk over the entire border. Stamp harlequin image with VersaMark onto scrap of Sheer Heaven. Chalk with lighter-color chalk. Allow to dry. Overstamp alphabet stamp on top of dried chalk with VersaMark and chalk with darker-colored chalk. Cut out harlequin and use as accent on page.

Second Page: Paint Sheer Heaven with texture paint. Let dry. Overstamp with an alphabet stamp. Cut out and apply to layout. Turn the pages into a flip chart with eyelets and ribbon.

LITTLE BOYS ARE MADE OF

BY LESLIE

Create background with cardstock and strips of patterned paper. Mat photo and stitch around the edge. Add word stickers to layout along with printed journaling. Punch circles from brown foam. Heat with heat gun, then apply white pigment ink to stamps and stamp dots or stripes into the foam. Sprinkle with clear embossing powder and heat set. Adhere circles to layout with adhesive dots.

giggles

AUTUMN

BY CATHY

Stamp images on small pieces of burlap with VersaColor ink. When completely dry, cover burlap with Mod Podge to seal ink and to prevent from "shedding." Punch holes in the top of each piece and hang from hemp.

CHAPTER FOUR

GALLERY

In the Gallery, our talented artists showcase their best work and show off some of their favorite techniques. Since gathering all the right supplies for stamping can be rather pricey, it's essential to use the stamps you have as many times as you can. Check out how one stamp could be used four different but stunning ways. Let these ladies tempt you with the latest ideas that will make an impression on your projects.

Make Faux Postage Stamps

FOUR
BY CATHY

Cut squares and rectangles with postage stamp scissors. Using low-tack tape, tape off the edges of the squares and rectangles and cover the centers with ink using direct to paper technique. Add various embellishments within each "stamp."

KATIE
BY LISA

Lie palette stamp facing up. Using a creamy white pigment ink pad, coat the entire surface with ink. Coat detail stamps with dye ink, and carefully stamp them directly onto the palette stamp. The effect will add dye ink and remove the underlying pigment ink. Detailed stamps work very well for this technique, but do not use letter stamps, as they will end up backwards. Once all images are added, carefully ink the outside edge of the palette with a darker pigment ink color for depth (here, brown). Huff (breathe) on the stamp to re-moisten, and press firmly on cardstock to create the image. Tear around the edge and adhere to layout.

CANDLES
BY JENNIFER M.

Use a candle that has solid color throughout. Candles with a rough outer surface work best. Stamp on small pieces of tissue paper with chalk ink. Lay tissue on candle surface and gently heat with heat gun to melt tissue into candle. Add embellishments.

MY BEST FRIEND'S DAUGHTER.
JOSEPH'S SISTER.
AIDAN'S FIRST BEST FRIEND.
THE CUTEST LITTLE GIRL I KNOW.
SASSY AND WILLFUL.
SWEET AS CAN BE.
SMART AS A WHIP.
LOVES SOCCER AND DANCING.
DOES A MEAN BRITNEY IMITATION.
FRIEND TO MANY.
THE 'KATIE' REFERRED TO WHENEVER AIDAN SAYS
"KATIE IS MY GIRLFRIEND!"

ABEILLE
BY CAROL

Scan and print photo onto ink jet transparency. Paint an oversized slide mount and stamp images with various colors of chalk ink. Overstamping light ink over dark inks and vice versa produces interesting shadows and highlights. Insert transparency into mount and add floral accent. Create a cardstock envelope slightly larger than the slide mount card. Paint and stamp over surface. Sponge white chalk ink over all surfaces. Add handle, vintage mini-envelope, accent and fibers.

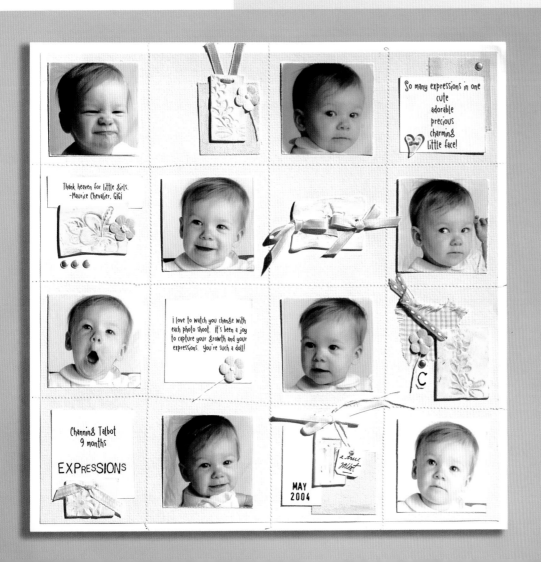

EXPRESSIONS
BY RENEE

Cut shrinky dink plastic into large rectangles. Heat until small, then immediately press a stamp into the plastic. Paint over hardened images with colors and add an overcoat of white wash. Machine stitch a grid pattern onto background paper and add various elements and pictures in each square.

Carefully poke tiny holes in both ends of eggs and blow out centers. Rub the outside of egg with while vinegar to help the ink hold better. Completely dry egg, making sure any water has drained from the inside. Attach stickers to egg. Using a make-up sponge, apply dye ink to egg and wipe off any excess.

EGGS
BY TRACY

FLY
BY LESLIE

Stamp butterfly stamp using red ink on both white and taupe cardstock. Trim and place at top and bottom of layout. Mat photo and embellish with a cameo pin tied with a butterfly charm. Add journaling and ribbon and sew along the seams. Cut title from white cardstock and stamp with butterfly stamp and black ink.

Your eyes sparkle as the stars, like the moon they glow
Your smile could light the world on fire, or did you know?
Your mind's full of everything that I want to know
I just had to let you know... I just had to tell you so...
You're my Butterfly, fly high ...fly, fly, fly

chloe raine lightfoot
photo taken on your 1st birthday
June 16th, 2004... FLY!

SURF'S UP
BY JENN B.

Layer patterned papers onto chipboard. Using paint as the ink, stamp image onto twill and attach to layout. For the surfboard, stamp the flower images and heat emboss with clear embossing powder.

Joe and Molly. Two of a kind but completely their own persons. They have been our friends since they were born and we loved watching them grow up. Molly is spirited and strong willed, funny and charming. Joe is easygoing and comedic, smart and caring. They feed off each others humor and constantly have me in stitches. Tripp and Patton have had a great time growing up with them too! Molly takes charge and they all follow along for the fun. Thanks for being part of our life!!!

PHOTOS TAKEN ON JUNE 15TH 2004 - JOE AND MOLLY

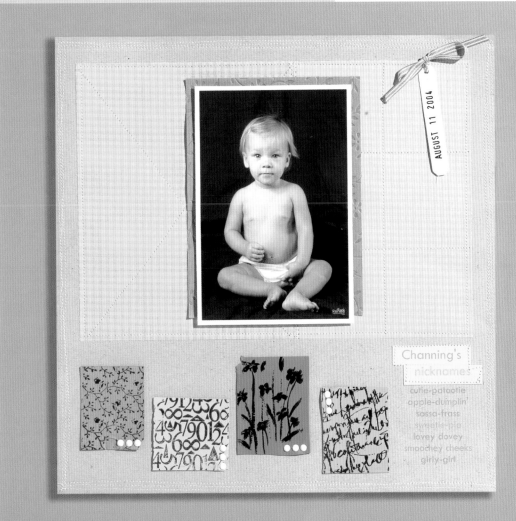

Stamp over Acrylic Paint

CHANNING'S NICKNAMES
BY RENEE

Pour acrylic paint into shallow plates. Allow to dry. Trim acrylic pieces into shapes, stamping images on top using StazOn ink. Print journaling onto page, adding a cardstock title. Attach patterned paper, sewing designs over them. Attach tag with ribbon.

AUGUST 11 2004

Channing's nicknames

cutie-patootie
apple-dumplin'
sassa-frass
sweetie-pie
lovey dovey
smoochey cheeks
girly-girl

my friend...

my brother...

my thanks to you for being part of US

MY BROTHER

BY JENNIFER M.

Use the following masking technique to recreate this layout. Stamp an image twice—once on final cardstock piece and once on scrap paper. Cut out image on scrap paper. Lay scrap image over final image. Stamp another image over the scrap, preventing it from overlapping. Do this on all the stamped images, including letters.

THERE HAS NEVER BEEN A SOUL HAPPIER THAN MINE WITH YOURS.

HAPPIER SOUL

BY JENNIFER M.

Arrange Hermafix squares in a diamond pattern as a page border or on a paper heart. Cover with embossing powder and heat emboss. To make the silver heart, cover paper heart entirely with VersaMark and emboss with silver powder.

TATUM

BY LESLIE

Mat photo on light blue cardstock. Place a letter sticker in one corner and embellish it with a flower and brad. Create background using strips of papers and ribbons. For the pink strip, temporarily adhere corrugated paper to a rolling pin. Coat generously with pink pigment ink or acrylic paint. Roll back and forth on light pink cardstock. Allow to dry. Using foam stamps and acrylic paint, stamp the images on another piece of cardstock and let dry. Hand cut the images and adhere on the stamped paper. Add faux stitching rub-ons to two of the paper seams. Frame title and journaling with a leather bookplate.

TATUM
...doing her part to make this world a cuter place to live in... age three

Companionable, interactive play. Building, stacking, sharing, helping. A collective effort between brothers, or shall I dare say it, friends. Two years apart, is sometimes difficult. For the elder does not quite understand how someone younger and weaker can commandeer such a wealth of parental attention. The past year has been an adjustment for all of us, now a family of four. Slowly and surely though, our two sons are building a genuine camaraderie. There has sparked a realization that a willing playmate has lived within our house this entire time. Though we as parents are often called to run interference, the affection is genuine, and the hours of play are endless. Trust me on this, you are both fortunate, for you have each other.

SIBLING REVELRY

BY TINA

Dye several strips of twill with colored fabric dye. When dry, stamp with ribbon stamps and VersaCraft ink (specifically for fabric). Stamp images on transparencies with StazOn ink. Cut the transparencies to fit inside metal rimmed tags. Thread the tags onto the twill with jump rings. Staple the twill in an overlapping fashion to the background.

Mix Ink Colors

SOFT PETALS

BY SHARI

Ink the stamp with your finger to get varied color. Spritz the rubber stamp lightly with water and stamp onto patterned papers, repeating the inking process between stamping. Tear the papers and mount over each other. Roll torn edges of the paper for a distressed look. Mount on card.

Stitch Around Stamped Image

DINNER TONIGHT

BY SHARI

Piece together several fabrics to make a mini-quilt. Stamp letters onto the fabric and hand stitch the outlines of the letters with black thread. Stamp letters onto the shiny side of shrink plastic. Punch plastic with a 1½" circle punch. Color the back of the circle with colored pencils. Shrink circle pieces with a heat gun.

WAITING FOR THE HURRICANE
BY JENN B.

Collage patterned papers to the left of an enlarged photo. Staple colored twill to layout. To create the small pogs, stamp images with StazOn and heat emboss with clear embossing enamel. Paint a small tag with green paint, then ink chicken wire with white paint and stamp over the painted tag.

MAGNETIC
BY TENA

Stamp on assorted found objects to create unique magnets. Mount thin magnet disks to the back of the objects using a strong adhesive like E6000.

Crack UTEE

ABC
BY TRACY

Paint patterned paper with Lumiere and let dry. Mount on cardstock to flatten as it tends to bend when drying. Ink some small pieces of patterned paper with chalk ink. Directly apply VersaMark ink to the tag and heat emboss with embossing enamel. Repeat inking and embossing a few more times. On the last time, quickly place an inked stamp into the warm embossing enamel and hold until the enamel hardens. Remove stamp. Repeat for all three letters. Carefully bend the tags to add cracks. Attach enlarged photo and embellishments.

Dave & Joyce ©/1953
First year of school together

Stamp letters onto cardstock strip. Use a craft knife to cut out the body of the letters or the centers if the letter is self-contained. Arrange various colored cardstocks and patterned papers behind the letters.

Cut Out Center of Letters

LOOK OUT, BAD GUYS!
BY LISA

"look out, bad guys!"

When does the obsession start? In the womb? No, even I know it happens when the first viewing of Teenage Mutant Ninjas occurs...or is it Yu Gi Oh? Teen Titans? Any of the above? What I DO know is this: Little boys are obsessed with Karate. Or just fighting bad guys in general. Whereas the boys of my generation played Cowboys & Indians, the boys of today are fighting green monsters, giants, and bugs that plan to take over the universe. All in good fun, of course. I actually considered signing Aidan up for Karate lessons at one point, but decided it might be a little too early to add any formality to his crime-fighting playtime.

On this particular afternoon, he wanted to show me his new moves (new from where?). Naturally, he asked if I would document them for posterity (in other words, he asked me to go get my camera!).

So these pictures tell the tale of my little bad-guy fighting boy. I wish the sounds of "Hi-YA!, Bam!, Take THAT!" could also be heard. You can imagine.

So all you bad guys, monsters, and bugs take note: There's a new crime fighter in town. 10/04

A-Z: things are always silly with you & me!

One thing is for sure – you and I are a goofy pair. We love to ham it up and act all silly. I love making you laugh, as do you. We can't just take a serious picture. Mine is more for a selfish reason: I look goofy in any picture, so it's best for me to just act goofy! ☺ You just enjoy following my lead. So, on this Easter morning, we just couldn't resist letting Melissa take a series of goofy shots of just the two of us. Brandon, I'm so glad you're my goofy picture partner!

2003

A-Z
BY RENEE

Stamp entire alphabet before cutting into individual letters. Sew around several letters and attach to background cardstock. Add fabric pieces and punched and inked hearts.

DUMBO
BY LESLIE

Create background with patterned paper and cardstock strips. Stamp musical notes in red ink and spritz with walnut ink. Stamp autumn definition and add to layout. Stamp letters for title, spritz with walnut ink, allow to dry and cut out. Assemble title below photo, adding child's name in between each letter of the title. Embellish layout with metal corner and hinges. Adhere journaling strip next to a length of ribbon.

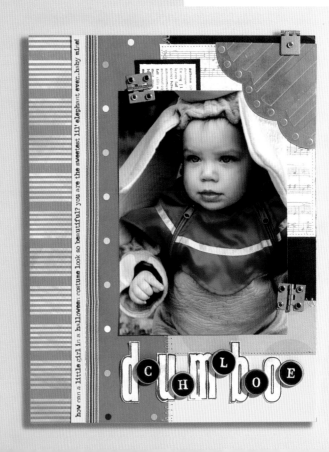

FLOWERS

BY JENNIFER M.

For the stitched card, stamp flowers with VersaMark and rub with chalk. Cut out petal portion only. Add to front of card with pop dots. Add stitching for stems. To make the torn card, stamp two flowers with VersaMark on two different pieces of white cardstock. Rub with chalk, using a different color combo on each flower. Tear strips from one of the flowers and glue over the other, lining them up. Stamp on an envelope with VersaMark and rub with chalk.

GETTING OLDER

BY PATRICIA

Line up four small tags with the punched holes facing opposite directions. Stamp flower onto tags, ink around edges of tags and add ribbon to top and bottom tags. Adhere photo, tags and ruler sticker to page. Cut patterned paper in a curved design and attach to layout at upper right and lower left corners. Print journaling onto transparency and place over tags, adhering the top under patterned paper. Machine stitch around the entire layout.

Emboss Images

GROWING UP
BY TINA

To superimpose the image of the stamped flower on the photo, stamp the flower in black on white cardstock. Scan the image at 300 dpi using the reverse image mode. Add image to a photo. The original photograph had a significant amount of black background, so the flower image was added directly onto the photo using photo-editing software. Print white text directly on the photo. Stamp the flower four times across the bottom of the white cardstock with black pigment ink. Heat emboss with black powder. Place epoxy letters over wavy strips cut from patterned paper. Layer a colored transparency over the background but not over the strips, then add the photograph on top.

HERO ARTS JAMAICAN FORGET-ME-NOT STAMP

Add Color with Alcohol Ink

GROW
BY TRACY

Stamp flower image onto a transparency with StazOn ink. Turn over and brush alcohol ink randomly over transparency. Cut to size and attach to page. Add squares and strips of patterned paper to layout. Using direct to paper, ink alphabet paper and stamp over the top with a flower and swirl. Cut large letter and attach with foam squares.

HOME

BY RENEE

SNOW CARD: Using StazOn ink, stamp arrows onto fabric. Trim around each image and add a chimney cut from fabric. Stitch tissue paper at the bottom to resemble snow and machine stitch smoke coming from the chimney.

CARDBOARD CARD: Stamp arrow image onto inked background and heat emboss with clear powder. Cut around each image and cut openings for windows. Attach to card front along with additional journaling.

CONGRATULATIONS CARD: Use direct to paper technique to create a blue background. Stamp arrow image over the top and heat emboss with clear powder. Cut around image and add two windows and a door cut from ledger paper. Ink additional papers, trimming into various shapes and attaching to card. Sew sun rays and make word strips for the title.

QUIRKY

BY JENN B.

Create background with strips of cardstock torn on one end. Apply rub-on stitches on the clean end. Staple strips of patterned paper over the cardstock strips. Cut negative holders into individual sheets. Print journaling and slip inside. Adhere the strips to the strips of cardstock. Collage photos on layout. For the arrow stamps, swipe pigment ink onto coated cardboard. Dry with a heat gun and stamp with arrow image. Cut around image and punch a hole on the end. Tie with ribbon and adhere to page.

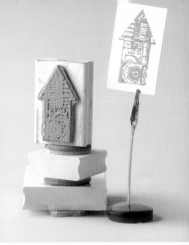

Did you know... of all The pups in The world (and There are a LoT of pups out There!) ThaT I Love you mosT?"

Ken overheard me say To Roxie in bed one morning.

MOST

BY JENNIFER M.

Stamp arrows in various colors. Cut out and adhere in a circle. Stitch through arrows for detail.

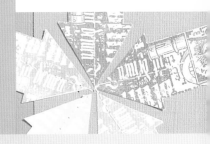

AL & JEN

BY TRACY

Using a brayer, apply dye ink to stamp, mixing colors. Stamp onto glossy cardstock and cut out around image. Attach photos and journaling block to page along with buttons, ribbon and other embellishments.

al and jen

We met Al & Jen when they moved in beside us on Cultus Court. What a blessing that was, as our previous neighbours thought clothing was optional much to our surprise (gasp). Jen is a scrapbooker too and we bonded instantly. Al is crazy and always makes us laugh. We all adore Feisal and his fetish for street hockey and all things trains. We would talk in the evening across the fence or through open windows. Good friends and neighbours indeed. The saddest part of moving to Mission was moving away from them. We now live about an hour away from each other (20 minutes if Dan is driving), and don't get to visit as much as we used to. Jen and I now email each evening, instead of meeting for tea and ginger snaps in our pajamas. Sometimes you meet people that you instantly know you will love. Al & Jen fit into this category (yes, even Al). They have seen us at our worst, seen our home in disarray and yet still like us.

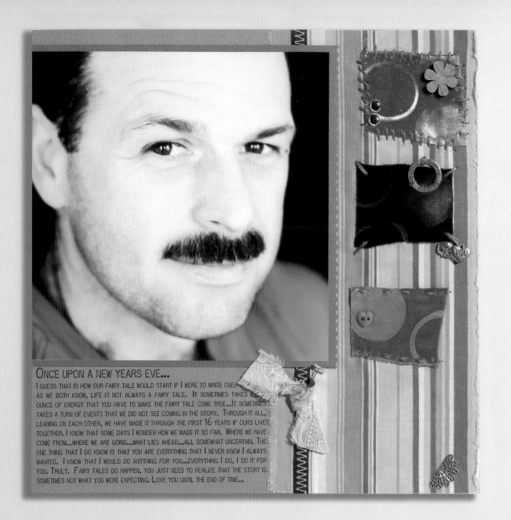

Heat Stamp on Velvet

ONCE
BY TRACY

Mat an enlarged photo and trim one edge with decorative scissors. To stamp on velvet, place uninked stamp face up on table and place velvet face down on the stamp. Using a hot iron with no steam, iron over stamp. Attach striped fabric to page with double-sided tape and stitch stamped velvet over the top. Embellish velvet with charms, buttons and a wooden flower.

Kiss Off Ink from Stamp

KEILAH
BY JENN B.

Using pigment ink, stamp circle stamp onto cardstock, then take a clean stamp (heart, dragonfly, etc.) and stamp on top of the circle to remove some of the ink. Dry with a heat gun and cut out circles. Punch holes and string together with ribbon to make a page border. Tie bows and trinkets to the ribbon and adhere to page. Randomly place other circles and cardstock strips to the page. Adhere quote with a safety pin tied with ribbon.

ELEVEN 0002004

You know you're sick when...

SMILE

THOMAS

EVEN BUBBLES CAN'T MAKE YOU

One point five weeks and counting. You are sick, your brother is sick, your father is sick. Unfortunately, you have seemed to take the brunt of it, fever, runny nose, generalized misery. In an optimistic hope of distracting you for a few moments, I whisked out your favourite thing, the bubble blower. As the bubbles rained down upon you, you attempted to humour me with some unenthusiastic batting. Then you simply laid down and collapsed in a heap upon the floor. The bubbles did not make you smile or laugh, instead today they made you cry. Nonetheless, I will continue my futile attempts to comfort you, because that is what mommies do.

Stamp with Paint

SMILE
BY TINA

To create the bubbles for the background, stamp the filled-circle stamp on the background with acrylic paint. Then stamp directly over top of the circle in another color with the outline circle stamp. Randomly add small circle rub-ons to background. Print journaling on a transparency and place over circles.

Stamp with Various Mediums

THANKS CARDS
BY TRACY

For the blue card, apply watercolor to stamp with a paintbrush, then stamp on cardstock. Let dry and embellish with buttons and greeting. Use a circle punch to make cutout on the front of orange card. Apply Twinkling H2O's to stamp. Stamp flower on inside of card so it shows through the hole. Stamp circles onto front. Let dry and apply small dots of Sparkles along circles and let dry. Embellish with a button. For the green card, paint wood letter with acrylic paint and let dry. Stamp circles on front with Perfect Medium. Brush Perfect Pearls powder over stamped circles. Brush off excess and spray with a fixative.

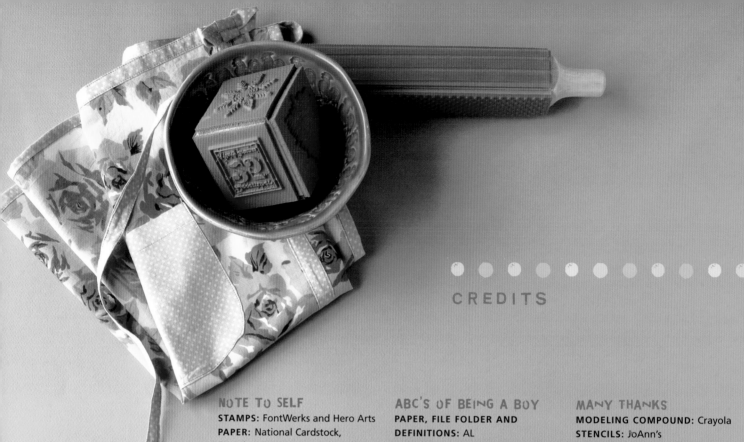

CREDITS

CHAPTER ONE:
STAMPS
PAGES 8-27

Alphabet

ALPHABET FRAME
STAMPS: Hero Arts
INK: VersaMagic and StazOn, Tsukineko

BABY GIRL
STAMPS: Li'l Davis Designs, Postmodern Design and Stamp Out Cute
RIBBON: May Arts
EMBOSSING POWDER: Ranger
INK: Ranger and Tsukineko

A MAMA AND HER LOVE
STAMPS: Ma Vinci's Reliquary and Stampabilities
INK: Nick Bantock, Ranger
PAPER: Basic Grey
LABEL HOLDER AND TAGS: Foof-a-la
TAB & RUB-ON: AL
SPIRAL CLIPS: 7gypsies
RIBBON: May Arts and MM

NOTE TO SELF
STAMPS: FontWerks and Hero Arts
PAPER: National Cardstock, 7gypsies, AL, K & Co. and MAMBI
FONTS: Constitution, Lean Tower, Serenade, Dreamboat, Gypsy, Professor, Heavenly, Libretto and Updated Classic, AL
SPIRAL AND TABS: 7gypsies
HALO CLOSURE: Cloud 9

ARTIST
STAMPS: Ma Vinci's Reliquary
PAPER: Rusty Pickle
FONTS: Outloud and Post Master, AL
RIBBON: Offray

FIRST DAY OF SCHOOL
FONT: 2Peas Weathered Fence
CHARM: Quest Beads
STAMP: FontWerks
STICKERS: Li'l Davis Designs and SEI
STENCILS AND POGS: AL
PHOTO TURNS: MM and 7gypsies

TIME WELL SPENT
PAPER: MM and AL
RIBBON: Marcel Schurman
STAMPS: Ma Vinci's Reliquary and Image Tree
RUB-ONS: AL
INK: Memories; ColorBox, Clearsnap; Nick Bantock, Ranger; StazOn, Tsukineko; Rubber Stampede

COLE
PAPER: The Paper Palette and Déjà Views
FONT: Worn Machine, AL
INK: StazOn, Tsukineko

ABC'S OF BEING A BOY
PAPER, FILE FOLDER AND DEFINITIONS: AL
STAMPS: Ma Vinci's Reliquary, Wordsworth, FontWerks, Postmodern Design, EK Success and Stampers Anonymous
LEATHER FRAME: MM
FONT: KeyBoard Plaque
INK: Nick Bantock, Ranger, StazOn, Tsukineko

Make Your Own

DEVOTED DANCER
INK: VersaMagic, VersaMark and VersaColor, Tsukineko; Memories
METAL TAG: All My Memories
STAMPS: Hero Arts and Postmodern Design
FONT: Cantabile
PHOTO: Daniela Berkhout

JUST BE SILLY
STAMPS: Stampabilities and Image Tree
PAPER: SEI, Sassafras Lass, Anna Griffin and KI
RIBBON: May Arts

RANDOM PICTURES
FONT: Handcrafted, AL
BLENDER PEN: JudiKins
INK: Memories
RIBBON: May Arts

SHOW CIRCLES
PAPER: AL, Paper Loft, K & Co.
RIBBON AND INK JET CANVAS: Memory Lane
BELT BUCKLE AND RUB-ONS: 7gypsies
"JOURNEY" PLAQUE: Maude & Millie
INK: ColorBox, Clearsnap

MANY THANKS
MODELING COMPOUND: Crayola
STENCILS: JoAnn's
FLEX FOAM: Fibre Craft
CARDS: Die Cuts with a View
RIBBON: Offray

SOMEDAY
PAPER: Basic Grey and K & Co.
EPOXY STICKERS: Li'l Davis Designs
CONCHOS: Magic Scraps
INK: Ranger
FONTS: Times and Times Again

NOAH
STAMPS: PSX Design
INK: StazOn, Tsukineko
PAPER: Carolee's Creations

BUTTERFLIES
INK: VersaMagic, Tsukineko
PAPER: CI

JOY
CRAFT FOAM: Darice
INK: ColorBox, Clearsnap
EMBOSSING POWDER: Hero Arts
PAPER: AL and Basic Grey
PHOTO TURN: K & Co.
HANDLE: 7gypsies

SARA AND CASE
STAMPS: Hero Arts
PAPER: NRN, MAMBI and Doodlebug
RIBBONS: May Arts
CHIPS: Bazzill
INK: ColorBox, Clearsnap

LEGEND

AL: Autumn Leaves
CI: Creative Imaginations
MAMBI: me and my BIG ideas
MM: Making Memories

Backgrounds

BLOCKED CARDS
INK: VersaColor, Tsukineko; Nick Bantock, Ranger
STAMPS: Hero Arts and PSX Design

ZEST FOR LIFE
STAMPS: Postmodern Design, FontWerks and Hero Arts
INK AND PEN: VersaMark, Tsukineko
EMBOSSING POWDER: Hero Arts and Ranger

MY PARENTS
STAMPS: MM and FontWerks
GESSO: Golden's
COLOR WASH: 7gypsies
METAL LETTERS: MM

MOMENTS
FABRIC PAPER: K & Co.
STAMPS: Hero Arts and Purple Onion Designs
EMBOSSING ENAMEL: Suze Weinberg
METAL PHRASE AND FLOWER: MM
WOOD FRAME AND METAL CHARM: Li'l Davis Designs
TWINE: Scrapbook Wizard
TWILL: Scenic Route

STANDING AT THE EDGE
PAPER: Paper Fever, AL, SEI, KI and Basic Grey
STAMPS: A Muse Artstamps, Hero Arts, Inkadinkado, Hampton Art Stamps and Ma Vinci's Reliquary
INK: ColorBox, Clearsnap; Memories
ICE CANDY: KI
FONT: Kravitz Extra Thermal

BUTTERFLY
PAPER: Jennifer Collection and Manto Fev
STAMPS: Magenta and Savvy Stamps
TITLE LETTERS: Foof-a-la
FONT: Initial
INK: ColorBox, Clearsnap; VersaColor, Tsukineko

DAVID AND MINNIE
STAMPS: Wordsworth, Stampers Anonymous, Hero Arts and Ma Vinci's Reliquary
INK: ColorBox, Clearsnap; Memories

TAB AND KNOCKERS: Foof-a-la
PAPER: AL, Chatterbox, Li'l Davis Designs, EK Success and Déjà Views
BUTTON: Jesse James
RESIN FLOWER: K & Co.
METAL FLOWER: All My Memories

23 DEGREES
STAMPS: Hero Arts, Penny Black, PSX Design and PrintWorks
INK: ColorBox, Clearsnap; VersaMark; Tsukineko
BRAYER: Speedball
BUTTONS AND STICKERS: American Crafts
STITCHED TIN TILE: MM

Found Stamps

SOMEDAY
PAPER: Basic Grey
STAMPS: Wordsworth and Stamp Out Cute
INK: VersaMark, Tsukineko; Distress Ink, Ranger
EMBOSSING POWDER: Ranger
BUTTONS: Coats and Clark
THREAD: Talon

FRIENDS
STAMP: Hero Arts
PAPER: National Cardstock and 7gypsies
RIBBON: Offray
CLEAR CANVAS: Magic Scraps

SAN DIEGO
ACCORDION BOOK: Lineco
BOOK CLOTH: Books By Hand
BOOK PLATE: 7gypsies

SUNSHINE
STAMPS: Hero Arts
INK: Brilliance and VersaMagic, Tsukineko
BUTTONS: Doodlebug
PHOTO: Sankey Price

DINOSAURS
PAPER AND TAG: Rusty Pickle
HANDMADE PAPER: The Artistic Scrapper
INK AND WALNUT INK: Tsukineko
LETTER STICKERS: MM
CLAY: Polyform Products

JUST BLOWIN' BUBBLES
PAPER: Chatterbox
FABRIC PAPER: K & Co.
RIBBON: May Arts
CIRCLE FRAME: Déjà Views
FONT: CK Chemistry

YOU
PAPER: Manto Fev
FONT: Cleanliness, AL

APPLE PICKING
FONT: 2Peas Weathered Fence

HAVE SPICES, WILL COOK
INK: ColorBox, Clearsnap; VersaMark; Tsukineko
PAPER AND BUTTONS: American Crafts
CONCHOS: Scrapworks
FONTS: American Typewriter and 2Peas Favorite Things

JOURNEY
STAMPS: Postmodern Design, FontWerks, Ma Vinci's Reliquary and Stamp Inks Unlimited
INK: StazOn, Tsukineko; Memories
ADHESIVE LENS SHEET: ArtLenz
CHIPBOARD LETTERS: MM
BOSHERS: Bazzill
STICKER AND PAPER: Basic Grey
LETTER TILE: Westrim

BOGEY
RIBBON: Scrapbook Wizard and Offray

CHAPTER TWO:
MEDIUMS
PAGES 28-51

Ink

BEAUTIFUL
STAMPS: Rubber Stampede and Postmodern Design
CONCHOS, PINS, FILE TABS, WAXED LINEN AND PAPER: 7gypsies
INK: Distress Ink and Nick Bantock, Ranger
FONT: Age Old Love, AL

GLASS ORNAMENTS
CHARM: MM
RUB-ONS: AL
ALCOHOL INK: Ranger
ORNAMENTS: Handmade Holidays

MERCY
STAMPS: Hero Arts, Stampabilities and Serenity Stamp
CORK: CI
INKS: Distress Ink, Ranger
FONT: Uncle Charles, AL
PHOTOS: Keith Chapman

DANDELION WISHES
PAPER: MM, Chatterbox and KI
RE-INKER: VersaMark, Tsukineko
EMBOSSING POWDER: Ranger
RUB-ONS: AL
FLOWER AND EPOXY NUMBER: Li'l Davis Designs
FONTS: 2Peas Journaling Dingbats, Pupcat and Steelfish
PHOTOS: Joy Bohon

MAKE EACH DAY COUNT
ALBUM: 7gypsies
TWILL: Ink It!
BRASS NUMBERS: Memory Lane
INK: Tsukineko, Marvy and Ranger
GESSO: Golden's
PAPER: MAMBI
MINI FOLDER: EK Success
STRING CLASP: K & Co.
STAMPS: FontWerks, Stampers Anonymous, MM and Li'l Davis Designs

I MISS YOU
FONT: 2Peas Weathered Fence
STAMPS: Hero Arts
STENCILS: AL
PAPER: MM
INK: ColorBox, Clearsnap; VersaColor, Tsukineko; Ranger
EMBOSSING POWDER: Paper Moon

V & A
INK: ColorBox, Clearsnap; VersaColor, Tsukineko
SPONGE ROLLER: Shur-Line
DIE-CUT LETTER: My Mind's Eye

DAISIES
PAPER: Chatterbox and Basic Grey
TWILL: 7gypsies

KISS
STAMPS: Savvy Stamps, All Night Media and Wordsworth
INK: StazOn, Tsukineko; Ranger
COLOR WASH: Ranger
PLASTIC CIRCLES: Little Black Dress Designs

Other than Ink

REAL BOY
PAPER: K & Co., Mustard Moon and KI
FABRIC PAPER: K & Co. and MAMBI
STAMPS: Hero Arts

TENDER LOVING CARE
STAMPS: Impress Rubber Stamps and Hero Arts
FONT: Serenade, AL
CLAY: Sculpy

SO ALIVE
STAMPS: Hero Arts and Purple Onion Designs
FONTS: Handcrafted and Patriot, AL

QUILTED FRIENDS CARDS
STAMPS: Hero Arts
RIBBON: MAMBI

PINKY SWEAR
STAMP: Postmodern Design
PAPER: K & Co.
PHOTO TURNS: 7gypsies
WOVEN CORNER: MM
FONTS: 2Peas Tasklist and 2Peas Style Magnet

THANK HEAVEN
STAMPS: Hero Arts and JudiKins
FONT: Uncle Charles, AL; 2Peas Fancy Free
VELLUM QUOTE: AL

TRANSPARENCY: Artistic Expressions
LEAFING: Fashion Flakes, Biblical Impressions
PAPER: AL
PHOTO: Jill Beamer

CATCHING SNOWFLAKES
STAMP: JudiKins
CHARMS: Carolee's Creations
PAPER: Basic Grey
FONT: 2Peas Weathered Fence

MY DAD
PAPER: K & Co. and MM
STAMPS: Bunch of Fun and Stamp Out Cute
INK: StazOn, Tsukineko
METAL PRONG FASTENERS AND CLIPS: 7gypsies
GLAZE: Paper Plus, Delta
METAL STRIP: Once Upon a Scribble
METAL STAMPS: Harbor Freight
FONT: Effloresce

BABY CARDS AND ENVELOPE
CARDS: MM
STAMP: JudiKins
RUB-ONS: K & Co.

BABY NO MORE
PAPER: Li'l Davis Designs and Rusty Pickle
LEATHER PAPER: K & Co.
DYE: Rit Dye
STAMPS: Li'l Davis Designs and MM
RIBBON: May Arts

RESIST TAGS
STAMPS AND TAGS: Hero Arts
PAPER: 7gypsies
INK AND DYE: VersaMark and VersaMagic, Tsukineko
EMBOSSING POWDER: Hero Arts

Resist

WISH FRAMES
RESIST INK: Ranger
INK: ColorBox, Clearsnap; Adirondack, Ranger
FONT: 2Peas Scrumptious
STAMPS: Hero Arts and Stampington & Co.

SMILE
STAMPS: Hero Arts, The Blue Hand, JudiKins, Postmodern Design, B-Line Designs, Stampers Anonymous, Wordsworth and Paper Impressions
INK: Memories; Adirondack, Ranger; VersaMark, Tsukineko

SIMPLE JOYS
STAMPS AND EMBOSSING POWDER: Hero Arts
PAPER: Mustard Moon
INK: VersaMark; Tsukinkeo

THE QUIET AFTERNOON
CANVAS: Canson
WAX CRAYON: Susan Scheewe
HEAT TOOL: Walnut Hollow
RIBBON: EK Success
STAMP: Savvy Stamps
INK: Hero Arts; Distress Ink, Ranger
RUB-ONS: AL

NEW LIFE
STAMPS: Postmodern Design and Leave Prints
INK: Resist, Ranger; ColorBox, Clearsnap
METAL FLOWERS: All My Memories

CARDS AND FOLIO
STAMPS: Stampington & Co.
ENVELOPES AND DOT CARD: Waste Not
RIBBON: Memory Lane and Ink It!
PEWTER CORNERS AND CHARM: Maude & Millie

PAPER: AL
INK: Tsukineko and Marvy
HEART FRAME: Scrapworks
RIBBON: Loose Ends
EMBOSSING INK AND POWDER: Ranger
BOOK JACKET: Memory Lane

ART SCHOOL— HERE I COME
STAMPS: Stampington & Co.
INK: StazOn, Tsukineko; PSX Design
LIBRARY POCKET: AL
FONTS: Retro, AL; 2Peas Cadence

Embossed

EVERY
STAMPS: Ma Vinci's Reliquary, Hot Potatoes and Stampa Rosa
INK: VersaMark, Tsukineko
EMBOSSING POWDER: PSX Design
PHOTO CORNER: MM

MUCH BETTER
STAMPS: Hero Arts, Paper Impressions and PSX Design
FONT: Cafecoco
ICICLE: KI
COVERED BUTTON: Junkitz
CHARM AND FLOWER: K & Co.
EMBOSSING POWDER: Powder Keg
TRANSPARENCY: Artistic Expressions

THINGS I WANT YOU TO KNOW
FONT: Old Royal, AL
TABS: AL
INK: VersaMark and VersaColor, Tsukineko
EMBOSSING POWDER: Hero Arts
METALLIC RUB-ONS: Craf-T
STAMPS: Inkadinkado and Hero Arts

C—I LOVE YOU

PAPER: MAMBI and SEI
VELLUM: SEI
EMBOSSING ENAMEL: Suze Weinberg
INK: ColorBox, Clearsnap
CHARM AND STENCIL: MM
METAL FLOWERS: Carolee's Creations

MINE

STAMP: Paper Parachute
INK: Memories
FONTS: Typewriter, P22; Typewriter-Regular, Voluta Script, Perpetua, Butterbrotpapier, Trajan Pro, Viner Hand ITC, Migraine Sarif, Stamp Act and ITC Garamond.
EMBOSSING POWDER: Hero Arts

FUN IN THE SUN

PAPER: Rusty Pickle and K & Co.
STAMPS: Great Impressions and Rusty Pickle
INK: Clearsnap
EMBOSSING POWDER: Creative Beginnings
TAG: Rusty Pickle
TACKS: Chatterbox

YOUR BROTHERS

FONT: Worn Machine, AL
STENCIL: American Traditional
INK: VersaMark, Tsukineko
EMBOSSING POWDER: Paper Moon

Digital

JKF

BRUSHES AND PAPER: Artist's creation
FONTS: Outdoors, AL; Harting and Depressionist Three

UP CLOSE & PERSONAL

BRUSHES, PAPER, FLOWERS AND TAG: Artist's creation
FONTS: Uncle Charles, AL; Scrap Cursive, Lettering Delights; Pharmacy and Crack Babies

MEXICO

BRUSHES, ACRYLIC PLATE AND STRING: Artist's creation
FONTS: Outdoors and Modern Type, AL
PLATE SPECIFICATIONS: Drop Shadow–Distance: 4 pixels; Spread: 0%; Size: 4 pixels. Inner Shadow–Distance: 21 pixels; Choke: 0%; Size: 42 pixels. Inner Glow–Overlay: Opacity: 30%; Noise: 0%; Color: Black; Elements: Softer; Choke: 0%; Size: 21 pixels; Contour: Range: 50%; Jitter: 0%. Bevel & Emboss–Inner Bevel; Chisel Hard; Depth: 250%; Direction: Up; Size: 16 pixels; Soften: 16 pixels; Shading: Angle: 120%; Screen: White; Opacity: 100%; Color

Dodge: White Opacity: 35%; Color Overlay: Orange Opacity: 44%.

SCHOOL

BRUSHES, FLOWER, PHOTO EDGES, PHOTO TURN AND HINGE: Artist's creation
FONTS: Pharmacy and Spacesuit

SISTERLY LOVE

BRUSHES AND PAPER: Artist's creation
FONTS: Old Remington, Highlight and Verdigris, AL; Times and Times No Roman

HAPPINESS

BRUSHES, PAPER AND OVERLAYS: Artist's creation
FONTS: Evening Stroll, Dreamboat, Charisma, Playbook and Old Remington, AL

M

BRUSHES, PAPER, SLIDE MOUNTS, CLEAR PLATE AND DOTS: Artist's creation
FONTS: Times, Selfish and Roughwork
SPECIFICATIONS: Clear: Drop Shadow–Distance: 7 px; Spread: 0%; Size: 4 px. Inner Shadow–Color burn: Black; Opacity: 45%; Distance: 31 px; Choke: 0%; Size: 42%. Inner Glow–Overlay: Opacity: 30%; Noise: 0%; Choke 2%; Size: 29%; Range: 50%; Jitter: 0%. Bevel & Emboss–Inner Bevel; Chisel Hard; Depth: 181%; Direction: Up; Size: 10 px; Soften: 16 px. Color Overlay–Normal Blend Mode: White; Opacity: 15%. Slide Mounts: Apply a custom shape (rounded square); Bevel & Emboss Style–Emboss, Smooth, Depth: 131%; Direction: Up, Size: 3px; Soften: 0 px.

MY EVERYTHING

BRUSHES, PAPER, VELLUM AND SLIDE MOUNTS: Artist's creation
FONTS: Scrap Cursive, Lettering Delights; Stamp Act and SF Old Republic
BEVEL AND EMBOSS STYLE: Inner Bevel: Smooth; Depth: 100%; Direction: Up; Size: 5 px; Soften: 0 px.

CHAPTER THREE:
SURFACES
PAGES 52-71

Fabric

REMEMBER

STAMPS: Hero Arts, JudiKins and Stampers Anonymous
INK: StazOn, Tsukineko
WOOD FLOWER: Li'l Davis Designs
EPOXY WORDS: K & Co.
PAPER FLOWERS: Savvy Stamps
WOOD TAGS: American Tag

THE HIKE

PAPER: 7gypsies and AL
FONT: Highlight, AL
RUB-ONS, CLEAR BUTTONS, FABRIC TIES, TAG AND TAB: AL
WOOD LETTER: Li'l Davis Designs
LEATHER: The Leather Factory
ENGRAVING TOOL: Walnut Hollow
STAMPS: Stampotique and Hero Arts
INKS: StazOn, Tsukineko; ColorBox, Clearsnap

COLLECTIONS FOLIO

RIBBON: Memory Lane
VINYL-BACKED FABRIC: Ink It!
STAMPS: Stampington & Co. and Ma Vinci's Reliquary
TEXTILE PAINT: Jacquard Products
BUTTON AND TAGS: 7gypsies
BOOK PLATE: Li'l Davis Designs
CHARM: MM

FRIEND

INK: Distress Ink, Ranger; Brilliance, Tsukineko
EMBOSSING POWDER: PSX Design
STAMPS: Hero Arts, JudiKins and Wordsworth

COURAGE

PAPER: AL
STAMPS: Hero Arts, Magenta, Wordsworth, Wisecracks, Savvy Stamps and PrintWorks
FONT: Uncle Charles, AL
INK: StazOn, Tsukineko

CITY GIRL

PAPER: Anna Griffin
RIBBON: May Arts
CANVAS FRAME: Li'l Davis Designs
STAMPS: Ma Vinci's Reliquary
TAG: Foof-a-la
BRAD BAR: Karen Foster Design

POLKA

STAMP: Impress Rubber Stamps
FONTS: 2Peas Variety Show and 2Peas Sitcom
INK: Memories

REMEMBER EVERYDAY

STAMPS: Hero Arts and River City Rubber Works
PAPER: 7gypsies and Hanko Designs
LEATHER: The Leather Factory
METAL FRAME AND PINS: MM
INK: StazOn, Tsukineko; Memories; ColorBox, Clearsnap

DRAGONFLY

STAMP: Plaid
PHOTO TURNS AND STICKERS: K & Co.
CHARM: Quest Beads
PAPER: KI
FONT: 2Peas Beef Broccoli
INK: Ranger

SILJE

STAMP AND MOLDING STRIP: MM
BEADS: Westrim Crafts

COWBOY IN THE JEANS

STAMPS: Postmodern Design, B-Line Designs and Rubber Stampede
PAPER: 7gypsies and Anna Griffin
RIBBON: May Arts
HINGES: MM
INK: Ranger
FONT: Anytime and Messenger, AL; Stamp Act

Clear

TRADEMARK EXPRESSION

BUTTONS: Hero Arts, AL and Doodlebug
STAMPS: Hero Arts
INK: StazOn, Tsukineko

DO YOUR PART

VELLUM AND VELLUM QUOTE: AL
STAMPS: Hero Arts, Magenta, Stampers Anonymous, Inkadinkado and Stampington & Co.
INK: StazOn, Tsukineko

CUTE AND SWEET

STAMPS: Hero Arts, Ma Vinci's Reliquary, Magenta, PSX Design, Postmodern Design, Stampers Anonymous, JudiKins and Rubber Stampede
BUTTONS: Doodlebug
VELLUM: SEI
FABRIC TIES: 7gypsies
SHRINK PLASTIC: K & B Innovations
INK: StazOn, Tsukineko

ENJOY EVERY MOMENT

FONTS: Verdigris, Post Master, Heavenly, Worn Machine, Afternoon Delight, Highlight, Old Royal, Modern Type and Eyewitness, AL; Typewriter, P22
CLEAR CD: Memorex
PAPER: Basic Grey
STAMP: Stampers Anonymous
INK: StazOn, Tsukineko; ColorBox, Clearsnap

GIRL TALK

STAMPS: Rubber Stampede
INK: StazOn, Tsukineko
MICROSCOPE SLIDES: Premiere
BLACK TAPE: Chartpak
FONT: Turtle Press
PHOTOS: Laurie Stamas

THE "NO" PARADOX

STAMP: Hampton Art Stamps
INK: StazOn, Tsukineko
STICKER PAPER: Heather's Stamping Haven
ALPHABET TRANSPARENCY: CI
PAPER: KI and Paper Fever
PETITE TABS: 7gypsies
RUB-ONS: AL
LETTER STICKERS: AL and CI

RUBBER GREETINGS
STAMPS: Hero Arts
PAPER: Daisy D's
INK: StazOn, Tsukineko

MY WORLD
SHEER HEAVEN: www.cre8it.com
CHARM AND BOOK PLATE:
K & Co.
WISH CHARM: MM
STAMPS: Purple Onion Designs, EK
Success, Green Pepper Press, Impress
Rubber Stamps and PSX Design
PAPER: Basic Grey
RIBBON: Memory Lane
INK: VersaMark, Tsukineko;
ColorBox, Clearsnap
KNOB: EK Success

LITTLE BOYS ARE MADE OF...
PAPER: Mustard Moon
STAMPS: Hero Arts
INK: ColorBox, Clearsnap
STICKERS: Pebbles and K & Co.

AUTUMN
FONT: Messenger, AL
CHIPBOARD LETTERS:
Li'l Davis Deigns
STAMPS: Hero Arts and Delta
TWIST TIE: Pebbles
INK: VersaColor, Tsukineko
PHOTOS: Lisa Grunewald

CHAPTER FOUR:
GALLERY
PAGES 72-89

Eye Candy

FOUR
STAMPS: Hero Arts, MM, JudiKins,
Stampendous, Savvy Stamps, Rubber
Stampede and Stampabilities
RUB-ONS: KI, AL and K & Co.
STICKERS: American Crafts and AL
"E": Li'l Davis Designs
Buttons and "princess": Doodlebug
INK: VersaMark, Tsukineko; Ranger
RIBBON: May Arts
CLAY: Sculpey

KATIE
STAMPS: Stampers Anonymous,
Magenta, Hero Arts, Paper
Inspirations and Hampton
Art Stamps
INKS: ColorBox, Clearsnap;
VersaColor, Tsukineko
PAPER: Basic Grey
FONTS: Afternoon Delight, AL;
Vintage ITC
PHOTO: Terry Chadwick

CANDLES
STAMPS: Hero Arts
INK: VersaMagic, Tsukineko

ABEILLE
SLIDE MOUNT : Foof-a-la
FLOWERS: MM
EYELET FLOWER: WooHoo
INK: ColorBox, Clearsnap
STAMPS: Stampers Anonymous and
PSX Design
HANDLE: 7gypsies
MINI ENVELOPE: Waste Not
FLOWER: Savvy Stamps
CHARM: Fancifuls
VINTAGE IMAGE: ARTchix Studio

EXPRESSIONS
SHRINKY DINK: Paper Moon
RUB-ONS AND TAGS: AL
FONT: 2Peas Chatter
FLOWERS: Savvy Stamps
STAMPS: Magenta
BUTTON: Buttons Galore
RIBBON: Offray

EGGS
INK: Ancient Page, Clearsnap
STICKERS: American Crafts,
Stampendous and SEI

FLY
CAMEO PIN: 7gypsies
PAPER: Doodlebug and SEI
CHARM: K & Co.
STAMP: Hero Arts

SURF'S UP
PAPERS: Rusty Pickle
TWILL: Creek Bank Creations
INK: ColorBox, Clearsnap;
Nick Bantock, Ranger
STICKERS: Rusty Pickle
STAMPS: FontWerks, Rubber
Stampede and Postmodern Design
RUB-ON STITCHES: AL

CHANNING'S NICKNAMES
STAMPS: PrintWorks, Savvy
Stamps and Wordsworth
PAPER: Daisy D's and
Jennifer Collection
INK: StazOn, Tsukineko
FONT: Uncle Charles, AL
TAG: AL
RIBBON: Offray

MY BROTHER
STAMPS: Hero Arts, Wordsworth,
Uptown Rubber Stamps, The Blue
Hand and FontWerks
INK: VersaColor, Tsukineko
FONT: 2Peas Tiger Tails

HAPPIER SOUL
STAMPS: Hero Arts, Stampourri,
Postmodern Design
PAPER: KI
EMBOSSING POWDER: Hero Arts
INK: VersaMark and
VersaColor, Tsukineko
FONTS: Uncle Charles, AL;
2peas Tasklist

CELEBRATE CARD
STAMPS: Hero Arts
INK: VersaMark, Tsukineko
TRANSPARENCY:
Artistic Expressions
EMBOSSING POWDER: PSX,
Powder Keg and Ranger

Surfaces

FRIENDS
STAMPS: Hero Arts
MAT FRAME: Kodak
INK: VersaMagic and
StazOn, Tsukineko
CARD: Hero Arts
LAMINATE CHIP: Home Depot

FINE LINE
STAMP AND SHADOW INK:
Hero Arts
BUTTONS: Buttons Galore,
Hero Arts and Doodlebug
FONT: Flighty, AL

MILK
STAMPS: Hero Arts
INK: StazOn, Tsukineko
EPOXY LETTER AND FRAME
CHARM: Li'l Davis Designs
WOVEN CORNER: MM
MIRRORS: Darice
FONT: Old Remington, AL

NECKLACE
LETTERS: MM
STAMPS: Hero Arts and
Postmodern Design
INK: VersaMagic, Tsukineko

GRANDMA'S BOYS
STAMPS: Technique Tuesday
and Stampers Anonymous
PAPER: KI and Rusty Pickle
RIBBON: May Arts
INK: StazOn, Tsukineko

WRAPPED BOXES
STAMPS: Hero Arts
INK: VersaMagic, Tsukineko

WILD WORLD
PAPER AND RUB-ONS: AL
STAMPS: Stampabilities and

Ma Vinci's Reliquary
INK: StazOn, Tsukineko;
Nick Bantock, Ranger
STICKERS: 7gypsies and CI
RIBBON: May Arts

GRIN
STAMPS: JudiKins, Hot Potatoes
and Hero Arts
INK: StazOn, Tsukineko
FONT: Messenger, AL
BUTTONS: Bazzill, MM and
Jessie James
EPOXY LETTER: Li'l Davis Designs
STICKER: American Crafts
TRANSPARENCY: CI
PAPER: My Mind's Eye
CHIPBOARD LETTER: MM
PHOTOS: Daniela Berkhout

THE SIMPLE STUFF
TEXTURE MAGIC: Delta
STENCIL: Plaid
INK: StazOn, Tsukineko;
ColorBox; Clearsnap
STAMPS: Savvy Stamps
and Hero Arts
PAPER: The Paper Palette
and Basic Grey
FONT: Worn Machine, AL

SAND & SEA
BOARD BOOK: Westrim Crafts
METAL CHAIN: Karen Foster Design
CHARMS: American
Traditional Designs
STAMPS: MM, Li'l Davis Designs,
Commotion Rubber Stamps

PENSACOLA BEACH
STAMPS: Li'l Davis Designs,
FontWerks and Rusty Pickle
TINY NOTEBOOK AND CHARM:
Global Solutions
PIN: MM
INK: Ranger

THE ONE PERSON
STAMPS: Hero Arts and
Stampers Anonymous
HEARTS: MM
INK: StazOn, Tsukineko

TATUM
MONOGRAM LETTER: K & Co.
PAPERS: Keeping Memories
Alive and AL
METAL FLOWERS:
Carolee's Creations
**LEATHER FRAME AND
STAMPS:** MM
RUB-ON STITCHES: AL
INK: ColorBox, Clearsnap
FONTS: Bankgothic and
Amertype Condensed

SIBLING REVELRY
TWILL: Creek Bank Creations
DYE: MM
STAMPS: Limited Edition
INK: StazOn and
VersaCraft, Tsukineko
FONT: GF Ordner Inverted and
Slightly Warped

SOFT PETALS
STAMPS: Hero Arts and My
Sentiments Exactly
INK: Watermark ink,
Tsukineko; Ranger
RIBBON: Offray
PAPERS: AL, 7gypsies and K & Co.
CARD: Die Cuts With a View
BOOK PLATE: MM
STICKERS: AL
METAL TAB: 7gypsies

DINNER TONIGHT
STAMPS: FontWerks
RIBBON: Offray
PAPER: Daisy D's
BOTTLE CAPS: Design Originals
INK: StazOn and
Brilliance, Tsukineko

WAITING FOR THE HURRICANE
PAPER: Anna Griffin, CI and
Karen Nuberger
POGS AND STENCIL: AL
STAMPS: JudiKins, Postmodern
Design, Inkadinkado and
Image Tree
EMBOSSING ENAMEL:
Suze Weinberg
FONT: Typewriter, P22
CHIPBOARD LETTERS:
Li'l Davis Designs
TWILL: Creek Bank Creations
INK: Nick Bantock, Ranger;
StazOn, Tsukineko

MAGNETIC
MEMO BOARD AND MAGNETS:
MM
STAMPS: MM, Stamp Out Cute,
Hero Arts, Stampers Anonymous,
Our Lady of Rubber, www.sun-
dayint.com and Limited Edition
INK: StazOn and VersaMark,
Tsukineko; Distress Ink, Ranger
EMBOSSING POWDER: Ranger

PLASTIC RECTANGLES:
Little Black Dress Designs
BOTTLE CAP: Mustard Moon
LEATHER FLOWER: MM
**WOODEN FRAME AND PAPER
FLOWER:** Prima Artist's Aids
**CHIPBOARD CIRCLE AND
COLORED WASHERS:** Bazzill
PAPER CLIP: Li'l Davis Designs
RIBBON: May Arts
PAPER: Anna Griffin

Versatility

ABC
STAMPS: FontWerks, All Night
Media and Inky Antics
INK: StazOn and VersaMark,
Tsukineko; ColorBox, Clearsnap
PAINT: Lumiere
EMBOSSING ENAMEL:
Suze Weinberg
**TAGS, PAPER AND STITCHED
LEATHER:** Li'l Davis Designs
LEATHER FLOWER: MM
EPOXY ACCENT: CI
CLEAR BUTTON: AL
PIN: Westrim
FONT: Messenger, AL

LOOK OUT, BAD GUYS!
STAMPS: FontWerks

A-Z
STAMPS: FontWerks, Hero Arts
and PSX Design
INK: VersaColor, Tsukineko;
Memories and Hero Arts

DUMBO
PAPERS: KI, 7gypsies and SEI
STAMPS: Purple Onion Designs
and FontWerks
TIN CORNER: K & Co.
RIBBON: May Arts
FONT: Modern Type, AL

FLOWERS
STAMP: Hero Arts
METAL PIECE: All My Memories
INK: VersaMark, Tsukineko;
Distress Ink, Ranger

GETTING OLDER
PAPER: Basic Grey and Pebbles
STAMP: Hero Arts
INK: Clearsnap and Ranger
STICKER: EK Success
RIBBON: May Arts
FONTS: 1942 Report;
Cezanne, P22
BOOK PLATE: K & Co.

GROWING UP
PHOTO: Shelley Rankin
PAPER: MM, Paper Fever and AL
TRANSPARENCY: CI
STAMP: Hero Arts
INK: Brilliance, Tsukineko
EMBOSSING POWDER: Ranger

EPOXY NUMBERS:
Li'l Davis Designs
CLIPS: AL
FONT: Fin and Broken 15

GROW
STAMPS: Hero Arts and JudiKins
BOOK PLATE: CI
INK: StazOn, Tsukineko; ColorBox,
Clearsnap; Alcohol ink, Ranger
FONT: 2Peas Yo-Yo
PAPER: Li'l Davis Designs,
Chatterbox, My Mind's Eye
and EK Success

HOME
STAMP: Stampers Anonymous
PAPER: Manto Fev
INK: ColorBox, Clearsnap; StazOn,
Tsukineko; Ranger
CARDS: Hero Arts and
The Container Store

QUIRKY
STAMP: Stampers Anonymous
RIBBON AND RICK RACK:
May Arts
INK: ColorBox, Clearsnap;
StazOn, Tsukineko
PAPER: KI and American Crafts
RUB-ON STITCHES: AL

MOST
STAMP: Stampers Anonymous
INK: VersaColor, Tsukineko
BUTTON: Doodlebug
FONTS: Hairbrained, AL

AL AND JEN
STAMPS: Stampers
Anonymous and FontWerks
BUCKLE: K & Co.
EPOXY: CI
INK: Adirondack, Ranger
FONT: Messenger, AL

ONCE
STAMP: Hot Potatoes
TRIM AND FLOWER:
Li'l Davis Designs
FONT: Old Remington, AL

KEILAH
STAMPS: Hot Potatoes,
Hero Arts, Cherry Pie and
Global Solutions
RIBBON: May Arts
METAL LETER: MM
DOG TAG: Chronicle Books

SMILE
PAPER: KI
STAMP: Hot Potatoes
INDEX TAB: AL
RUB-ONS: AL and KI
STICKERS: Mustard Moon
and CI
FONT: 4KeyCourier and
Love Letter

THANKS CARDS
WATERCOLOR POWDER:
Twinkling H2O's
**PERFECT PEARLS AND
PERFECT MEDIUM:** Ranger
STAMPS: Hot Potatoes and
Impress Rubber Stamps
WOOD LETTER: Walnut Hollow
SPARKLES: PSX Designs

STAMPS USED AS BACKGROUND IMAGES ARE AS FOLLOWS:
A MUSE: www.amuseartstamps.com,
Page 20
ALL NIGHT MEDIA:
www.plaidonline.com, Pages 33, 58
B LINE DESIGN:
www.blinedesigns.com, Page 59
CLUB SCRAP: www.clubscrap.com,
Page 23
FONTWERKS: www.fontwerks.com,
Pages 68, 69, 77
HERO ARTS: www.heroarts.com,
Pages 19, 21, 34, 35, 41, 55, 60, 65,
71, 77, 80, 85
HOT POTATOES:
www.hotpotatoes.com, Page 88
IMPRESS:
ww.impressrubberstamps.com,
Page 57
JUDIKINS: www.judikins.com,
Pages 16,18, 28, 31, 32, 37, 52, 67,
70, 72, 79
JUST FOR FUN: www.jffstamps.com,
Page 25
MAGENTA: www.magenta.com,
Page 74
POSTMODERN DESIGN:
postmoderndesign@aol.com,
Pages 6,18, 36, 39, 42, 78
RUBBER STAMPEDE:
www.deltacrafts.com, Page 62
STAMPERS ANONYMOUS:
www.stampersanonymous.com,
Pages 21, 74, 86
STAMPINGTON & CO.:
www.stampington.com,
Pages 43, 56, 75

DESIGNING WITH STAMPING is newest addition to the impressive Autumn Leaves **DESIGNING WITH...** series that includes the following titles:

DESIGNING WITH VELLUM

DESIGNING WITH NOTIONS

DESIGNING WITH TEXTURE

DESIGNING WITH PHOTOS

DESIGNING WITH WORDS

DESIGNING WITH SIMPLICITY

DESIGNING WITH FABRIC

THE BOOK BOOK

DESIGNING WITH PROJECT CALENDAR

QUOTE, UNQUOTE: VOL.1

QUOTE, UNQUOTE: VOL.2

Thanks for letting us fire your imagination with ideas to satisfy your creative palette. Relish your copy of **DESIGNING WITH STAMPING** and watch for more extraordinary books in our flagship series.